“Today You Choose”

“...Either You Serve Me or You Serve The World...”

My Story

Ken Metherel

ISBN: 149758583X
ISBN 13: 9781497585836

Prologue

I met God one day in 1979. I didn't know I needed Him in my life. I was my own God. For over thirty years I had lived for one reason only and that was to satisfy my own desires. He changed my everything in a split second. I hope my story will help guide someone who is walking on a similar path as I was to come to a personal relationship with Jesus Christ. No matter what you have done or who you have hurt, God sees you as His own, giving you the opportunity to walk with Him forever. It is in your hands as He says

"TODAY YOU CHOOSE"

Dedicated to
all my friends who were a part of my life at
WHITE ROCK CHRISTIAN FELLOWSHIP
We are family

Book One

Chapter One

My Best Four School Years Are Spent In Grades Eight And Nine

"It could only happen to you!" Patsi exclaimed between tears. That morning I had the idea to start to write my story and thousands of thoughts were rushing through my mind. But first a coffee and two pieces of toast before beginning. With toast ready, I moved into the living room to meet with my laptop and comfy chair. I sat the laptop on the ottoman and the toast beside it only to have toast one slide off the plate and, with cheese, jelly and all, land upside down on the carpet. I then sat the plate with the second piece of toast on the shelf beside the chair where it decides it wants to go onto the floor with the other piece - what a mess" - toast, jelly, drops of butter, and my composure all laid out on the floor. Patsi quickly responds with "Ken It could only happen to you"

Welcome to my world, won't you all come in?

My life has been one of craziness, filled with a lot of adventure, love, anger, joy, faith, pain, resentment, and a huge dose of humor. I have lived in Europe, Quebec, Ontario, Florida, British Columbia, Manitoba, and Arizona.

I have been a soldier, salesman, and an auctioneer. I have owned furniture stores, a fish and chip business, liquidation stores, and an online book business. I have raised llamas, beef cattle, kids and a whole lot of hell.

I have flown airplanes, thrown grenades, visited brothels, been in jail, skied in the alps. I have been poor and wealthy, won and lost fist fights and poker games, raced motorcycles and cars, and a whole lot more.

I made history in my first week of life. I was born in Peterborough Ontario on January twenty sixth, 1947. My parents were married at eighteen and I came along when they were twenty. I was born with Pyloric Stenosis. The bottom of my stomach was closed and I could not digest food. Every time they fed me, I threw it back at them with force. (I made up for that in later years)

My mother was sent home after a couple of days while I was left behind in the hospital wondering..."Where's the beef?"I don't know how they kept me alive. I was told that my parents were called and told that they needed to come to the hospital to sign papers as I needed an emergency operation or I would die in a few hours. I'm glad the car didn't break down. I was opened from top to bottom and the doctors discovered the problem. It was the first successful operation of its kind in Peterborough, Ontario - I think there should be a plaque or something.

My earliest memories are of dogs, lots of dogs, licking my face. I have seen a picture of me in a crib with about a dozen puppies, so I guess that is where it comes from. My childhood was complex as my father had anger problems and he seemed to be mad at someone or another a lot of the time. He often was angry with my brother or me and usually expressed it with words or occasionally with a severe spanking.

My mother tried to create some security for us but really wasn't successful at it as she had to deal with him as his wife more than as our mother. After a particularly tough time when my father was having a nervous breakdown, my mother had to pack up my brother, my sister, and me to sit in the car outside his workplace so he could go to work.

She told me one time that she couldn't love me because she had to love Dad. I really don't believe she didn't love me, but it was something that a young boy didn't need to hear. I guess they were in some kind of counseling and she got the message mixed up.

My mother had a brother Cliff who died in a truck accident when she was sixteen. He had been a strong influence in her life and she was really rocked by his loss. Her mother was a wonderfully kind Christian lady. As a family they attended a Plymouth Brethren Church near Young's Point, a small community about twenty-five miles north of Peterborough. When my mom was sixteen, she rebelled and moved to Peterborough with a girl friend, where she met my Dad.

My dad grew up with his twin brother Jack and younger sister Anne. His life was one of privilege but was filled with turmoil. He fought with his brother on a daily basis. Most often it was physical battles as they were both of the same character. My grandmother showed a lot of preference for her daughter Anne, often taking her on special trips, leaving Jack and dad at home. On one occasion she only took Anne to Port Hope to see the Queen, leaving the boys behind. Anne was always allowed to use the family car, while neither of the boys was. It sort of explains some of my father's anger. He was always looking for some recognition but it was never to come. His upbringing was to affect all our family for all of our lives. He experienced rejection as a child and carried that into his adulthood He never was able to express his true feelings. It was to be carried on for the next generation.

My grandfather was around thirty-four when he married my grandmother. He had fought and been gassed in the First World War. He was a Sergeant Major in the Signal Corps. He never talked about the war, but there was a gas mask and an Enfield rifle hanging on the wall in their cottage. When he left the army he joined Canadian General Electric as a draftsman and by the time we were around he was the department head

Discipline of the boys was left to my grandmother who wasn't very good at it. She was, however, a very wise investor so that by the time we kids came around, they owned a mansion on a hill that was divided into five large apartments, a row of townhouses, and about twenty-five acres of land with large cottage along Chemong lake, just north of Peterborough.

My dad's parents were not very happy with him marrying my mother and as a result he was often at odds with them. Another real problem was how my grandmother treated my mother. It was awful. She was shunned by her and by my dad's sister Anne.

My mother was under a lot of pressure, but she found solace in her mother. All was thrown into despair when her mother had a fatal heart attack in 1953. Mom lost her one place of safety and was left to deal the Metherel assault alone.

Her father then married a spinster very soon after. His will was changed and when he died in 1971, my mother was left nothing. The family farm was left to the stepmother who passed it on her nephew. How she dealt with all of this I don't know, but she did the best she could.

The life in our home was often crazy. There were so many battles between my parents. Fortunately, there was no physical harm to my mother that I knew of. The worst I saw was when my mother was leaving the home with a suitcase in one hand, tears streaming down her face, and my father screaming at her to "get out". We kids were in hysterics and forced to sit on the couch and watch our mother leave. After a while my father put us into car and went to find her. She was walking down a highway. My father pulled up beside her and soon the family was back to our form of normal. This repeated itself on a few occasions, always with the same result.

I was never to play catch or go for a walk with him. When I was just a toddler he would wrestle and tickle my brother and me. It ended when Hal fell off the bed during one occasion and broke his shoulder blade. Dad bought me a bicycle when I was about eight but left it to a friend of mine to teach me to ride. He loved to fish and hunt. He took me with him occasionally. We would have to sit quietly, as we waited for hours for a bite or for any ducks to fly near. When I declined to go one time, I was never taken again. He taught me to shoot a twelve gauge shotgun when I was about ten. I never really understood the seriousness of the weapon and almost killed my brother when he took us after rabbits behind our home. I didn't have the safety on and when I tripped it went off. Thankfully, Hal was a little behind me as I blew a hole in the ground.

I can remember a few funny times. On one occasion my mother had made a butterscotch pie for my father, his favorite, but when my father came home they quickly got into a loud argument. It ended with my mother chasing my father out of the house with the pie in hand. She let it fly just as my father ducked. The pie flew over his head and landed on the side of the family car. Our dog quickly took advantage of the situation by licking the remnants from the car.

On another occasion my father had promised my mother a new set of dishes. They had saved the money and finally the day arrived to buy the dishes. My mother waited for my father to come home but when he came in he told her that he had changed his mind and wanted to buy something else. She blew up and solved the problem by taking every dish in the house and smashing them on the kitchen floor. The new dishes were in the cupboard the next day.

We did not have a Ozzie and Harriet life. There were some times of calm but they were rare. My father was a master carpenter and built us some fantastic toys over the years. He handmade a bobsled, a huge teeter-totter and even a life size TV camera. The best time each year was during his two week vacation when we would go camping on a sandy beach near Barrie's Bay, Ontario. We would pitch a tent next to the beach at a resort owned by family friends, Helen and Carl Pitts. Our days were filled with swimming, (I learned when I was pushed off a raft) catching huge frogs and just plain having fun with other kids. The hard part was going trout fishing with my parents. Dad could only put in two lines as we were using metal line go deep in the lake. Mom would sit in the front with the three kids sitting in the middle. We would leave home early in the morning and fish until dark. It was at least twelve long, boring hours sitting on a piece of 1" x 12"wood seat. On one occasion my mother had reeled in her line to re-bait it when somehow the rod went over the side. The hook caught the side of the wooden boat so the next hour was spent watching my father wind the 400 ft line around a beer can until he retrieved the rod. I don't know if that is the day but we have a picture with us coming home with 33 keepers.

Another day, my father let someone drive his sea flee (a small flat bottom, one person racing boat that was about ten feet long). There was a dead man's throttle so that if a driver was thrown out the boat would shut off. This person didn't connect it and he hit a big wave that sent him ten feet into the air, landing well behind as the boat carried on at full speed, pilotless. There was such a panic on the beach as every boat chased after the driverless boat. The first job was to keep it away from the driver until they could pick him up, and then to try and guide it toward a safe spot on the shore where it could be beached on the sand. A boat would get beside it and bump it in the direction they wanted to go. It took about thirty minutes of excitement to finally see that flying piece of plywood aim for the sandy shoreline. It was heading in at about forty mph when it hit the shoreline, motor roaring. It flew like an airplane before landing sliding over twenty five feet, coming to a stop against a tree. My father quickly ran up and turned the motor off. He actually let me drive that boat when I was a little older.

Hinterland Beach was a paradise for our family. It seemed like another world filled with happy memories. We three kids were exploring one day when we came upon a hornets' nest. It became a run for your lives situation and I got a whooping because my brother was slower than me and got the worse of it. Each day Helen would bake bread to sell from the little store they had to supply the camp. At eleven am each day you would find a group of kids waiting at the back door of the store where Helen would come out with slices of hot bread, buttered and covered in homemade jam. It was gifts from heaven as it melted in your mouth. I can still remember the taste of that bread sixty years later. My parents had saved over the year for the holiday and allotted each of us a small daily allowance to spend on a pop or ice cream. Best of times were spent at Hinterland Beach each year.

One of my father's first jobs after the army was selling vacuums door to door, something I was to do later. He told of us not having food in the house as he went out to sell one day. Talk about pressure to make a sale. He succeeded and we ate that night. He was far from lazy and always was trying different ways to make money. He had been a partner with Carl Pitts in a boat building business based in our barn; It didn't work out so then he tried raising chickens only to have them all die as chicks. That was followed by a successful chicken plucking business only to have the barn blow down by hurricane Hazel in 1954. I remember how a green pickup truck would pull up to the barn with cages of chickens piled high on the back. Out would pile a mother and father followed by a girl about my age who smelled real nice. The cages would all be unloaded at the far end of the building. It was a real production line until at the end you would have featherless raw chickens to pack up and take home. My favorite part was the pucker machine. It was a rotating barrel with hundreds of rubber plugs sticking out. As you held the chicken against the barrel, the feathers would all be grabbed by the rubber, pulling them all until the bird was naked. It was a slow and cumbersome job but it was a lot better than doing it by hand.

Another venture was growing Christmas trees. He hired the boy scouts to come and plant a thousand trees in our back field. I was old enough to help in this one and we worked all day in the hot sun. You would dig a small hole, plant the tree and then cover it over with dirt. One after another, tree after stinking tree, all day long. They grew for a few years until a neighbor's bonfire spread into the tree lot and destroyed them all.

His last venture was with a neighbor selling RV trailers on the property across the road from us. It started to require more time then he could he afford and he quit. Of course, this business went on to be successful as H& M trailer sales. (M was Metherel).

My father joined the volunteer fire dept and he excelled at it. He soon had a trailer hitch put on his truck so he could tow the fire trailer. (They didn't have a fire truck, just a trailer) He soon was made a captain of the dept and a few years later became the chief. The fire dept grew from the lone trailer to having a large fire hall built across the road from our family home. It was equipped with a tanker truck, a pumper, and a first response vehicle all under my father's leadership. All these years later as I write this I realize how privileged I was to be able to ride in the trucks and even standing on the back, hanging onto the bar across the top, as we raced to fires. I was often given a water back pack and told to kill any small fires before they spread from the major fires. My father kept the position for about forty years until he had a stroke in 1993. He had to call it quits and it drove him crazy as he would watch the trucks leave the hall without him. Today, His name is on the hall. It is called THE D.A. METHEREL FIREHALL in Otanabee Township just outside of Peterborough.

When school days started with grades one thru eight in a one room school, Mrs. Amy Hudson was our teacher. This senior citizen was the meanest person in the world. She would hit me on the knuckles with the edge of a ruler, pinch my ears, and make me sit in the corner with a dunce hat on. I somehow survived this new assault, but when my brother came in the next year it quickly got much worse for him. His big "mistake" was that he was left-handed and that was not acceptable for dear Amy. She would not let him use his left hand with the expected results. My brother failed grades one and two. He was damaged goods when he went into school and a complete mess after she finished with him. He was so screwed up that by fifteen he had discovered drugs with crime starting by age twenty; ending with Hal spending the rest of his life being in and out of prison. He went missing at the age of thirty after having messed up his mind up on every kind of drug possible.

The only thing good thing I remember about school happened in about grade five or six when the school was doing a fundraiser by selling tickets for a raffle. We each were given five tickets to sell. I went around the neighborhood and sold my tickets and brought the money back the next day. I was the only one who had sold them all so they gave me five more and they were sold right away too. Soon I was selling all the tickets and I was called "Ken the Salesman". For the first time I knew who I was - I WAS "SALESMAN". I HAD AN ID AND WAS RECOGNIZED FOR IT. It was the first of many life changing events.

We lived on a small ten acre farm outside of town, next to a much larger farm. One day, when I was twelve or thirteen, I awoke to find the field next door filled with 100's of Shetland ponies. It was every kid's dream.

My friends and I soon were building corals in the woods where we would round up some of these ponies and attempt to ride them. We had little success, but we had a blast trying.

The barn at that farm was renovated into an auction barn and a whole new world opened up for me. They held auctions each year for these ponies. Buyers from all over North America would bring pockets full of cash, ready to buy these wannabe horses. It was like a circus to me. Excitement, color, nervous horses, people yelling - everyone was on steroids. I watched for the first two days and on the third day when a ring man missed a buyer's bid, I yelled for all I was worth, and the auctioneer heard and saw me. It was another life changer because he made such a big deal of it. After winning that bid, the same buyer would only give me his bid and I was yelling my head off. Soon the auctioneer was telling me to chase other bids and I was running all over the auction ring and yelling – "YA" – "RIGHT HERE" – "MY BID". I was a novelty to the crowd. I was a kid in a man's world. The auction owner told me how good I had done and after that I was asked to work at every auction. He gave me $5.00.

A photographer from the Toronto Star was at one auction. He took my picture and interviewed me. I was told it was printed, but I never got to see it.

I was having a hard time in school with getting a grip on concepts. Things didn't make sense to me, just like my home life. In grade eight, I was really struggling and I got the strap from the principal regularly. It hurt like crazy, but I didn't cry. Not there - Not then. I was always small and overweight. I didn't have the nerve or the knowhow to fight and paid a big price for it. I was bullied, taunted and called names. I hated being held in class, so to escape I started to make myself sick. I would put my head down on my desk and stick my finger down my throat. Up came lunch and I went home. After the fourth or fifth time my mother took me to the doctor. That ended that idea.

Once, while watching the bigger kids play baseball, I was too close to the batter and got hit in the head with the bat when he swung. I got a three inch cut in a round shape around my left eye. I still have the scar.

Another time when one of the baseball teams was short a player, I got to play in the outfield. A screaming drive was hit towards me and I made a great catch. What a great feeling to have the school hero tell me, "Great catch, Metherel"

I really tested my mother's love when my best friend Larry and I were building a go kart on the second story of the shed that was attached to our house. We had finished the kart and decided to paint it. My father had left a half full, five gallon pail of gun metal grey boat paint on the ground level. We saw no reason why we couldn't use some of it for the kart. There was a ladder attached to the wall that we climbed to get to the upstairs. I grabbed the pail of paint and raised it above my head to pass up to Larry who was about half way up the ladder. He was to grab it and raise it up to the floor above him. All went well until Larry grabbed the pail in some way that caused it to dump the paint. It cascaded onto my head, then down onto my shoulders until I was covered. We didn't know that oil based paint wasn't washable, so the only solution for me, I thought, was to get into the bathtub as fast as possible. I raced for the house, running thru the porch, when I realized I was tracking paint from my shoes. I tossed the shoes off, continued thru the kitchen, around the corner, down a short hall to the bathroom. As I turned, I saw the footprints I was leaving from my paint soaked socks. I started to panic as I jumped into the tub, turned the water on with it not having any effect on the paint. My fear grew into terror as I tried to rub the paint from the side of tub. I was a dead man. My mother was at work when Larry dialed the number telling her what had happened. She was home in less than ten minutes. She calmed me down as we started the clean up by getting out the turpentine. It was with great care she removed the paint from my head and face. My clothes were thrown in the garbage. May hours later the house was evidence free and father never knew what happened to his paint. He may have wondered about the large colored section below the ladder but it was never mentioned. Another debt I owed my mother that went unpaid.

My parent's relationship was one centered on my father's moods. He often revealed outrageous fits of anger. He would get mad at my mother and she would react back. I don't ever recall them talking through a problem. It seemed like every Sunday morning there was a war. My father must have done something the night before to tick mom off and away they would go. It always ended up in a screaming match. I don't know how they resolved problems, but somehow life went on.

I started to notice girls around this time and was totally shy around them. There was a girl that I had been in class with since grade one. All of a sudden she looked different. I stared at her whenever I could and went so far as to write in a schoolbook that I liked her. What a mistake that was when it was found the day we turned in our books. The whole school soon knew my secret. I was made to sit in the classroom and clean the book as a penalty. Janet, the object of my dreams, came in the class and asked if I knew where something was. I turned red as she acted as if nothing was wrong.

By this time I was old enough to babysit my brother and sister. They often would act up and then mother would go off on me. One time, as punishment, she got a girl I knew who was a year older than me to babysit all three of us. It destroyed any confidence I had as it was soon news in school of what a loser I was.

I was very good at marbles. We all had a collection of marbles in the 50's and mine were kept in a purple felt bag. I cherished my collection and always wanted more and better ones. We would play different games for our marbles. Sometimes it was for fun but as I got better, keepers became the rules. I now was a gambler and won more often than not.

It went from marbles to hockey cards. We would all stand facing a wall, throwing the cards towards the wall, and whoever's card was closest got to keep the cards "...the joy of victory and the agony of defeat." If only I had kept those cards. Today they, along with all the other hockey memorabilia I collected would be worth a lot.

I was always looking for ways to make some spending money. I sold worms for fishing up at the corner near our home and picked bottles. I tried selling lemonade from a stand without much success. The occasional person would stop out of pity and drop a nickel in the cup. The hardest I ever worked was when I picked rocks in a local farmer's field. The same farmer used me to sell his produce door to door. Each Saturday morning we loaded up his truck and took a load of veggies to town. I would then go from house to house with an apple basket full. I got to meet a lot of people and sold lots of stuff. I became a lot more outgoing and gained confidence to talk to strangers.

I got a newspaper route with the Toronto Star and Star Weekly. It was spread out so far because I lived in the country that it was impossible to deliver to the homes, even by bike. I saw the local store had a rack for people to pick up the local Peterborough paper and I soon was stuffing my Toronto papers in the box. The storeowner was a friend of my parents and never told me to stop. It saved me hours of work each day. The paper had a contest to see who got the most new customers. I worked hard and had thirteen by the contest end. The prize was a new ten speed bike and I had my thirteen entries in the box. Judgment day came and they called out a name, but it wasn't mine. I was so sad until I learned the name was of one of my new customers. Did I ever look good on the nicest bike around!

The manager for the paper soon had me working with other carriers to get new customers. I don't really know how I was able to sell so well, but I think it was because I was afraid of rejection. If you said no to me it meant you didn't like me and I couldn't handle that so I would keep asking until you said yes. It worked well and of course there were some rejections, but as long as there were lots of sales I was ok. After I joined the army the newspaper manager told my parents he had planned to for me to have a career working for the Toronto Star. When I had finished school he hoped that I would work from the Toronto office. I will never know how that would have turned out.

Life at home was always in turmoil. I recall after one particularly bad time being punished for something my brother had done because my father always said I was older and was supposed to stop him. I remember crying in my room and calling out to God, "Why do I have to live like this? This is wrong!" It was a very strange thing for me to say because I didn't know the first thing about God. We were sent to Sunday school each Sunday morning, not a far walk from our home. We were never told much about who Jesus was or why he came to earth; we just sang songs and played games.

Within the next year or so my mother took me to a very formal church in Peterborough. I was bored with having to stand up and sit down, having to kneel down and stand up, and listening to some guy in crazy clothes read from an old book, telling us how to live our lives. Something about that turned me off and I told my mother so as we left. I never went back and only attended church services when made to in the army. It took God another twenty years to get through to me.

That same Sunday school was the reason for one of my best lessons in life. My best friend Larry and I were often short of money. We both knew there was a small tin of coins in the Sunday school room where everyone put in the exact amount of pennies as their age on their birthdays. Larry and I often were in trouble together so it didn't take long for us to figure out how we could get some fast cash. We circled the building, looking to find a loose window and soon were inside. We found the tin and emptied it into our pockets. If that wasn't bad enough, we then made a heck of a mess with all the craft supplies (a technique we had learned to express our anger from breaking into the school the year before). With the money in hand our brains finally kicked into gear and we realized that we could not spend the money without being questioned about how we got it. My mother worked at the corner store so that was out. Being "wise for our age" we quickly decided to copy the cowboys on TV and to bury the loot. We found a spot next to the wall of the barn at Larry's house.

All was well for about two weeks until Larry decided to share our caper with another friend. This kid had a higher moral temperament then we did or wanted to get us in trouble, so he went home and told his parents. They then told Larry's parents and the next thing I knew, I heard the whistle blow (my mother's method of calling us) and I ran home. I opened the door and there standing around the table was Larry, his parents, and my parents. There was no question that the gig was up but Larry had decided to deny it. I walked into the room and my father asked "did I rob the church"? I confessed and doomed my friend. I was sent to my room while my parents decided my fate. Larry was beaten severely (his father was as physical as mine and maybe even a little more). I avoided the beating by having told the truth.

My punishment was another of life's lessons that actually changed me. My parents showed great wisdom by having me pay back the money I stole. Each Saturday morning, with my allowance in hand, I walked over a mile to the home of the little spinster lady who was in charge of the Sunday school. I would hand over my cash as she looked me in the eye. Each trip took forever and my shame grew with every step. It took six weeks at fifty cents per week to repay the money.

One day a local kid who was as tough as nails was beating me up. It was ridiculous how much of a wimp I was. I went home and told my father - BIG MISTAKE. He told me that if I didn't go out there and beat the kid up, he was going to beat me himself. I was trapped and went outside and told the kid that I needed him to run so that I wouldn't get beaten by my father. He turned and ran and I followed. And then something happened in me. A light went on and I actually chased him for real.

When I caught him I released a lot of pent up anger by putting a beating on him. Later that same day I found another guy who was always picking on me and gave him a licking too. What a wonderful day.

I always tell people that my favourite four years in school were the ones in grades eight and nine. I get lots of laughs when they hear it but there was much pain behind the veneer. After my brother repeated grades one and two my turn at failure followed when I failed Grade eight. I actually had the grades to pass but the teacher convinced my parents that I was too immature for high school. I repeated it only to score exactly the same grades. I didn't mature too much either in that year so it was a waste. In grade nine I attended French class for the first time. I "knew" that a different language needed a new alphabet so I zoned out for the first while. I woke up too late finding out English and French used the same alphabet.

I then failed French and that made me have to repeat Grade nine; I was lost again.

My sister Anne was a majorette and went for baton lessons every week. I never paid any attention for many months until there was a competition at a high school in Peterborough. My mother made my brother and me come with her and my life changed again. There were 100's of teenage girls in short skirts and tight tops running all over the place. I found a new favorite pastime that day when many of them stopped to talk to me or just smiled. Each corps performed as a group and marched around performing manoeuvres while a set of drummers kept a beat for them. It didn't take me long to figure out that the best place for a guy was behind one of those drums. I told my mother that I wanted to be a drummer and soon my evenings were filled with me beating a rubber pad, "PAR-A-DIDDLE – PAR-A-DIDDLE". I never got good enough to play a snare drum, but I could keep the beat so I became the tenor drummer. Four guys and fifty girls - OH YA! We practiced every week, but the best was on weekends when we would often travel to competitions. There was one particularly cute girl who took a liking to me and would always sit with me on the bus. She would cozy up tight and close and I finally understood what life was really about. I was far too shy to do anything about it, but it sure made me know that I really liked girls.

Chapter Two

Hup Two Three Four It's The Army Life For Me

I escaped Peterborough by joining the army at sixteen in a special program they had called the Soldier Apprentice Plan. I had been prepared for this by having joined the army cadets at fourteen, going to summer camp for six weeks at fifteen, and then joining the militia at sixteen. I had seen a poster at the armory describing life in the regular army and the Soldier Apprentice Plan. The program was to bring young men with leadership potential into the army at age sixteen. You would attend high school in the mornings and do military training each afternoon. I sent in an application with a letter giving my parents approval and was told to come to Ottawa for entry exams, etc. I scored very high in the IQ tests and the logic exams (good thing they didn't check on maturity). There was only one space left with over fifty applications for it and I got it.

I was sixteen and a member of the Canadian Armed Forces. I left Peterborough on a Greyhound bus on an August morning bound for Ottawa and my new life. I later learned that my mother cried all day after I left, but she was stoic as she watched me get on board, waving good bye.

I really don't remember how I felt about leaving home. I was so confused about life by this time, I didn't really know up from down. I now know that I was a wreck, but back then I was just blind to it. One report from my time at cadet summer camp said that, "Metherel couldn't see the forest for the trees." I do know that I was excited to start a new life.

I drank my first beer ever after arriving at the depot in Ottawa. A guy who was being discharged took me to Hull, Quebec, just across the river from Ottawa, to a pub that didn't check ages too closely. I found a new way to cope and escape. A few more beers were to follow. I was in Ottawa for three or four days before being sent to the COD in the east end of Montreal. I met a girl there and we went to a movie. It was my first time getting to first base. Oh, the army life had begun.

In Peterborough I had never seen a real black person, only on television and they were portrayed as servants. Upon my arrival at my shack in Montreal, I was told to go outside, line up, and wait to go to the quartermaster store to get my uniforms. I was waiting there when a tall black corporal told me to come to attention and marched me to the store. I was in awe as I saw how smart he looked in his uniform and in shock when we got to the store and heard the quartermaster refer to the corporal as "Whitey". I later learned that his name was Chuck White from Nova Scotia. He was to be my platoon corporal for the next two years.

We were thrown out of our beds at six each morning by the duty sergeant storming down the halls screaming at us. If one of us was a little slow to react, his cane found its way to the end of our steel frame bed, sounding like a thunder strike at your head. We had to make our beds in a very particular way; we were inspected each morning at our bedside as we stood at attention. The sergeant would always find something wrong and you were berated with a lot of foul language as he would tear our beds apart, making us redo it before we could start the day.

We would march or run everywhere we went. We spent hours on the parade grounds and were subjected to a lot of screaming in our faces if we were out of line or missed a step. The penalty was often to have to run around the parade ground several times with our rifles above our heads. Not much fun but we got fit in a hurry. We went to school each morning from eight to twelve, had lunch and did military training each afternoon. Lights out was around 10:30pm with most of us being exhausted from the day's work, followed by three hours of shack cleanup; spit shinning our boots and brass, ending with ironing our uniform for the next day. We also had to do our laundry and homework from school.

We were taught to shoot all kinds of weapons, even smg's (machine guns), and to throw grenades. I received my cross rifles and crown as a marksman. I had good eyes and a steady hand. Not many of us qualified and I was proud to wear the badge.

We were put through gas mask training where we put on our masks, entered a small, windowless shack filled with tear gas. After a minute or so we were made to take our masks off and take a big breath before we were allowed out. We would all try to hold our breath as long as possible but it always ended the same for everyone. A long exhale followed by our lungs filing with gas. It was such a shock to your system with mucus instantly forming in your mouth, your eyes on fire and panic ruled. We ran for the door, bursting into the sunlight as we all puked out our guts.

Later in the course we were taught to drive all sizes of vehicles from jeeps to deuce and half's (2 1/2 ton cargo trucks with auto transmissions). It was my favorite part of training as we wheeled these green monsters around Quebec roads. I did real well in this kind of training, but not so well in the "parade square" crap.

Our platoon had about thirty guys. The army's idea is to take any form of individualism out of a man and instill the concept of being a soldier and a part of a unit. "All for one and one for all". We were all proud to be a part of Forty Platoon buying corps jackets that matched. We wore them whenever we left camp. I never had a best friend while in the apprentice program. We all were just a part of a unit. The pay was sixty dollars a month until we were seventeen when it doubled to $120, as we were no longer considered boys.

After six weeks we were given our first pass, a four hour time away from camp. We were in our first year and several of the second year guys (it was a two year program) took us to a pub in downtown Montreal where we could drink. In those days you could order a beer by the quart and so to prove our manhood we all did. I only drank one but several of the guys had two. We were all pretty smashed when it came time to head back to camp. We headed out to St Catherine's street and boarded a bus going east. The bus, as all buses do, rocked and rolled, slowed to stops, and accelerated. This motion magnified the upset stomachs of some and before too long one guy leans over the next seat and pukes all over a lady in a fur coat. That set off a sequence, where one guy then another then another would start to gag and then puke. There were guys hanging out of every window and many throwing up on the floor. The bus came to screeching halt. We were all thrown off to the accompaniment of cursing in French from the poor driver who would have to clean it all up. As the bus started to leave one of our guys started to chase it. He was banging on the back door. The driver stopped and opened the door. Our guy leaned over the steps to retrieve his false teeth from the floor. It made memories for all of us and I'm sure the driver never forgot either.

Life at camp continued as normal until we got a two week pass to go home for Christmas. My father's attitude had somewhat changed toward me. He never stuck me again but the infamous "look" was still in his repertoire and was used often. His eyes would narrow as he would focus his distain on me. It was as far from a look of warmth as you could ever get. It made me feel worthless. I hated that look.

I returned to camp in January to more military life. Several guys had been thrown out of the course. One for fainting when getting a needle, another for lending money at one hundred percent interest for two weeks, and another when he got caught dressing up as a woman in downtown Montreal. He hid it real well as we were all very homophobic.

Because I had played the tenor drum for the majorette corps at home, I was recruited to play the bass drum on the apprentice band. I wore a large leopard skin over my uniform and marched in many parades all over Montreal.

There was an article in the Star Weekly News Paper about the Soldier Apprentice Program during my time in Montreal. It described us as the best fed, best dressed, best trained, juvenile delinquents in Canada. It wasn't far from the truth.

Life was not easy for me as a 'green monster' (the army term for us... the first year we were referred to as 'gobs'). I was five feet four inches and

140 lbs. when I joined and I didn't know how to fight. Many of the guys were much bigger and some had been boxers or learned to scrap on the streets. For the first year I was pushed around and really didn't get any respect until much later while in Germany.

My schoolwork was marginal and I didn't shine as a soldier either but somehow I was able to stick it out.

It finally came time for "trades training" for the last three months of our two years. My aptitude tests had shown I should be a clerk accountant (one who keeps track of military stores and handles the procurement of more goods as they were required). This was long before computers. It involved a lot of paperwork. It was quite complicated. The course was the hardest of all the ordnance corps training and had the highest failure rate. Almost half the students failed the course and were sent to other training that required less math skills. I somehow shone like a star in this course. I loved the detailed trail of paper and could grasp the complex purpose of each sheet. I aced the course with an 87% and was second only to one guy. My military instructors were in awe and could not understand how I could have such a hard time with the simple things we were suppose to learn and yet rise to the top where others had failed.

Graduation came after two long years. We were now regular soldiers in the Canadian Army with a trade and a posting. On graduation day hundreds of parents and others gathered from all over Canada to celebrate our accomplishments. My parents couldn't drive the 300 miles from Peterborough and it really did hurt, especially at the end when we all threw our hats in the air and the other guys were surrounded by well-wishers.

I was given a thirty day leave and a temporary posting in Montreal, to assist in officer summer training. It was only a thirty day job near a small community with a resort that catered to Jewish families from New York and Montreal. I met a Jewish girl who had come to the resort on her own. She was about my age and we hit it off. We spent a few hours' together and made plans to see each other later in the week. The day came but I was stuck on duty in camp. All the officers and NCO'S were away and my hormones were in action. I wanted to meet up with my little Israeli so

I stole a deuce and half truck, and started on my way to the resort. I was coming down the mountain so I could see a long way ahead on the road. I spied an officer's jeep as it turned onto the road heading towards camp. I knew I was in big trouble if they caught me with the truck. I found a spot to turn around and raced back to camp, beating the jeep by about a minute. I parked the truck and ran to my tent, diving into my cot, pretending to be asleep. I was told later that my flame had been asking where I was...a missed opportunity for this guy to "become a man".

My permanent posting was at camp Petawawa in northern Ontario, just above Algonquin Park. I was posted to 2 OFP (Ordnance Field Park). An OFP's role was to be prepared to carry all the stores that a fighting unit would need in the field. We were mobile in a series of trucks with each carrying a certain segment of the supplies. As a clerk accountant my office was in the back of a truck that was setup with desks, file drawers, etc. We were to be ready to go to war on very short notice.

As a private I was given other duties on a rotating basis. I had to wash dishes and peel potatoes in the officers' mess. I would serve as guard for our compound, having to spend the night alone in a locked compound.

I had a 1955 Chevy by this time and was always short on gas. One night, as I was on guard duty at our company compound, I parked my car next to an army truck near the back fence and was siphoning gas into my car. A car pulled up to our compound, honking its horn. My heart stopped. This would be a serious charge with time in the brig if I was caught. I left the car and hurried up to the gate to let him in. It was an officer who needed to go into his office for something. I couldn't breathe until he left, without discovering my crime.

Life was much different as a regular army soldier than as an apprentice. We were allowed into the mess (the army term for bar in camp). The army believed it was better to let us drink in camp rather than go into the bars in town. Beer was cheap, cold and plentiful. Many guys became alcoholics due to the policy of easy access to an unlimited amount of drink without any real judgment for drunkenness. All that was required was to just be able to show up the next morning to do our jobs.

The year in Petawawa was big. This boy became a man after meeting up with a town floozy at a local bar. A whole new world opened up to me and a new purpose - to find and sleep with as many girls as possible. I sucked at it. I had two different girlfriends who were willing, but I was so innocent I couldn't make it happen. By the time I was shipped out to Germany after a year in Petawawa. I had had a couple of experiences but was still very naive.

One evening while in camp at the mess, the pay phone rang and I was closest to it. A voice of an angel spoke asking to speak to someone in particular. I hollered for him, but he was not around so I struck up a conversation with the voice. Her name was Anne. I just knew she looked like Raquel Welch. Anne and I hit it off. She invited me to come to her place as she was alone and lonely. It didn't matter to me that it was twenty below zero with a blizzard blowing; I was going to meet this girl and now. It took almost an hour to drive the twenty miles to town and find the address. It was not in the best part of town. I had to go around to the back and up some stairs to meet Anne. I knocked on the door. It slowly opened to expose the wicked witch of the north. This girl was so ugly, she would scare dogs away. I mean it was warts and all. I turned and ran to my car. I learned something important about blind dates made over the phone and never wanted to experience that again. It was a long drive back to camp.

I asked to be sent to Germany in the spring of 1966. I received orders and was to be shipped out in August of the same year. After a thirty day leave I reported to the military air base in Cobourg, Ontario for my flight. I had flown in a small plane as a kid, but this was a new experience. It was to be a twelve hour flight in a prop plane over the Atlantic Ocean. I was a little nervous and my parents were of little help. I saw a machine where you could buy life insurance for two dollars. I showed it to my father and he replied with a smirk that he already had a couple bucks riding on me. We loaded the plane after many goodbyes. Single guys were put in the rear of the plane and I soon learned why. The engines were so loud you could hardly hear any talking. It was deafening. We all had headaches by the end of the journey.

We landed in Dortmund and were bused to our new camp. This one was 4 OFP in Soest, a medium size town in the British sector of northern Germany. This was just twenty one years after the war and the military was still run by NATO.

I was met at camp by some friends from Montreal and was taken to the local pub. In Germany they are known as gasthaus's. They are small beer houses that serve the local beer and outstanding food. There are many drinking games in Germany and that night I learned the first one. There was a tradition to pull a trick on a guy when it is his first time in the bar. All the gasthaus have a large glass boot that is used in the first game. The boot holds about five pints of beer and is passed around the table with each guy taking a drink. The game is that whoever drinks the last of it causes the guy behind to buy the next boot full. The strategy is to never drink too much so that the guy after you can't drink it all or if you are in doubt, you drink it all. It's not too hard to get hammered especially with German beer. The glass is in the shape of a cowboy boot and if left with the toe pointed up, the beer will explode out when air gets into the toe. The new guy never knows this and is covered in beer for the rest of the night.

I settled into my job and life in Germany with little difficulty, but I had a co-worker who, unknown to me, had it in for me. I had come out of my shell in many ways and now had a lot of friends and was getting more popular in the shack. My corporal was a friend from Montreal and it seemed like I was on fast track to get promoted. This co-worker decided he would sabotage my work by making many errors in the math on the order forms and then sign it with my initials. My corporal pointed the errors out to me and asked what was up. I couldn't explain why I was making so many errors, but there were my initials on it, so it seemed to prove it was me. I was moved out of the office and put into a desk that was front of an officer's office. The errors ended, but I could not explain what had happened. Many years after I left the army I was told what the guy had done. The guy died early in life so I never had a chance to confront him about it.

Another guy in our unit had a car and so he took three of us to Amsterdam for the weekend soon after we arrived. It was to become my weekend retreat for the next three years. The Dutch love all Canadians as we liberated them in 1944. Here it was twenty one years later and we were still treated as kings. We often couldn't pay for a beer, as the Dutch would take turns buying us round after round.

And then there was the "red light district". All along the canals would be row upon row of small windows with a door beside them. Each window would have a beautiful girl offering her wares. Girls of every nationality and color, most in their early twenties, would present themselves in as provocative dress as possible. The cost was twenty guilders ($5.00) and many a young innocent Canadian boy lost his virginity on Canal Street.

We were all kids with a lot of money in our pockets (we were paid about 400 dollars a month by this time) and with this opportunity of a sex market, the combination was irresistible to us. Sex became a commercial transaction and solved in a few minutes. We could go out to the bars, party for hours, visit Canal Street, and go back to the hotel. Amsterdam was only a few hours from camp and I'm sure I was there at least one weekend a month during my three years in Europe.

Life in Germany was going great but being stuck in camp without wheels was a drag. Some of us would get together and take a cab to town on most weekends but I wanted to be on my own. There was a guy in camp who wanted to sell a 250 cc Honda motorcycle. I bought it and started to explore the area around Soest. The Mona Sea Dam (made famous in the movie "The Dam Busters") was just a few miles away. The German roads were narrow and twisty, creating a great place to ride. It was fun for a while, but I soon grew tired of riding alone all the time. There were other guys in camp with big BMW motorcycles who I got to know, but my bike could not keep up with them. There was a guy returning to Canada who had a little red Renault with a sliding roof, which I bought for 300 dollars.

While in Germany we were given six weeks of holidays each year and usually broke them into three, two week periods. A friend named John

Chenier and I decided to head to France for two weeks of camping and exploring. We left Germany and drove nonstop until we got into the south of France. We arrived in Marseilles in the middle of the night after having driven what seemed like forever. We saw no campgrounds and came to a dead end, with a fence blocking our way. We stopped, threw the tent over the fence and set it up. We crashed right away and only woke when we heard voices outside the tent. I stuck my head out in the bright sunshine to see a group of kids standing in a circle around us. In the background I could see nothing but blue. It was the Mediterranean Sea, shining in incredible brightness, and only made all the more incredible because we didn't know it was there. We had set our tent up in the backyard of a beautiful home on the edge of the sea. We thanked the people and drove away.

We left there and travelled along the Mediterranean coast, eventually getting to Monte Carlo. The wealth there was evident right away. There were huge yachts in the harbor and nothing but high-end cars parked around the town. I tried to get into the casino and got as far as walking into a section where table games were played. The place was full. What I remember most is one Arab sheik playing with the biggest chips you could imagine. They were each the diameter of a small brick. I have no idea of their value, but he had a stack of them and many on the bet line.

On the way I had the idea that if a person could double up his bet he would win every two or three plays. We could not play in the casino because we were not twenty-one, but there was a form of roulette on the outside of the casino. It turned out to be similar to a carnie game at any county fair. In a short half hour we were near broke. We had only gas coupons and a minimum of cash to get back to Germany.

I checked the map and saw we were only a short distance from Italy and that there was a major road back into Switzerland from there. We crossed into Italy and found the closest restaurant and ordered pizza. The patrons looked at us like we were nuts. Pizza is an American food, but they made something similar but without cheese, hoping to satisfy us. Pizza without cheese is like spaghetti without sauce. My first taste of Italian food didn't work but it sure improved over the years.

Later that night we camped by the side of the road. We awoke this time shivering with cold, finding ourselves high up a mountain. We could see forever. It was awesome. The sun was bursting over the peak of a far off mountain with rays spread all over the valley, bouncing off the snow like crystals. The next day we went through a long dark, two lane tunnel going from Italy into Switzerland. We made it back to base without any further mishap.

Life in Germany was a little different than on the base in Canada. Our army duties were more important as we were nearer to potential trouble areas in the world. We had to be better equipped and ready for action. The cold war was in full swing at that time so we spent much more time in the field. We would work with the British troops and the Germans. We were preparing to fight the Russians.

On one field exercise we were on the move from one area to another. It was a late move in the middle of the night. It came as a surprise to us. A bunch of us had snuck off to a local gasthaus for a few brews earlier in the evening. My truck mate and I took another dozen in a bag to go. When the call for a move came in we were plenty bussed, but we sure couldn't let anyone know. We were to drive a 3/4 ton, so we loaded our gear and the remaining beers into the cab and formed up into a caravan to move to our next location. I drove first while my pal had a couple more beers. Then he took over and I fell asleep. I woke up and looked over to see my friend sound asleep at the wheel, his hands locked in place and his foot on the gas. I looked up the road to see that we had crossed over the centerline and had a pair of truck headlights coming right at us. I yelled, grabbed the wheel, pulling it my way and avoided disaster. We were dead men!! How did I wake at that exact moment? Only God knows. That was the first of many close calls I was to have.

One of the men in our unit had a twin brother in an armored unit. An armored unit used tanks and APC's (armored personal carriers – vehicles that were used to carry twelve to fourteen soldiers into battle to avoid enemy rifle fire). This guy was woken one night and told his brother had been killed. He was so distraught. In the morning he was informed it was an error. Another guy with the same last name was the victim. The most incredibly terrible thing then happened the next night when his brother was actually run over by an APC and killed. The mother was brought over to attend the funeral later that week. I left Germany in June of 1969 and during the week I left, three of our guys were killed in an airplane accident while doing jumps. One of the guys was the twin whose brother had been killed.

Each of us was warned about driving and drinking in Germany. The roads were much more narrow and twisty than in Canada. I came away without having an accident much to the surprise of many. Another guy in our unit wasn't so fortunate. His name was Hector Bournaville. Hector was a different kind of guy. He was a screw up of the highest caliber. He was so slow that he sometimes came for inspection with his coat buttoned wrong, with one button at the top missed or he hadn't shined his boots. Army Basics 101 were a problem for Hector. We called him Hanky. Well, Hanky saved up and bought an old car and went out to a bar on his first night. He didn't make it home as he wrapped it around a tree. Another mother had to go to Germany to bury her son. It was a very moving ceremony with us all in dress uniforms, a twelve gun salute, et al.

My move to an office that contained army clerks and civilians proved that I knew my job. I stayed in this office for the next year and half. There was another soldier in the office that lived in my shack, Bill Kalenchuck, a native kid from Saskatchewan. He had been adopted by a Ukrainian family when he was very young. Bill was a tough guy who had won a Golden Glove boxing competition as a teenager. I first met Bill in Montreal at a poker game where I won a good chunk of his cash. He didn't like me and I was afraid of him. In the same office there was a real cute Canadian girl working, whose husband was in another unit. When it came close to Christmas, she knew that it would be hard for single guys to be alone, so she decided that she would have Bill and me over. Christmas day arrived and they came to camp to pick us up. As we got in the car I noticed that

Bill had bought a gift for them. I was sick as I brought nothing. I tried to entice him into sharing the gift but without success.

We spent the day with them and had quite a bit to drink. After dinner we all went to a bar and drank even more. Bill and I were pissed by now and I decided I would call home. I made the call, collect, but could only say hello (there was a nine hour time difference). It was a bad idea because I soon became super home sick. I was kind of teary as we headed back to camp. Along the way Kalenchuck gets sick and pukes in their car. We stop. Bill gets out and somehow gets lost! He got lost in the middle of a road in Germany! We all get out and can't find him. They drove me back to camp and Bill did not show up for another two days. I learned much later that he had arranged for a woman that he had met in the bar to follow us. He had a better Christmas night then I did.

Both Bill and I had a competitive spirit and loved to gamble. We played high stake crib, "manna au manna", for the two years I was in Soest. I would imagine we broke even after thousands of games, but I smashed him in the women dept. On one occasion he had a hot date lined up with a beautiful blonde we both knew. When Bill was late for the date I quickly moved in. Can you imagine the thrill of victory when I woke him one morning and told him to look in my bed? His lost love looked up at him and he quickly made his way back to his stall.

Bill had a mean streak, particularly for me. (I don't know why.) He was tough and everyone knew it and respected him for it. He would torment me whenever the occasion arose. On one evening, as I lay in my bunk, he came by with his belt hanging from his hand. He flicked it, using it as a whip at me and then started to actually hit me. I will always remember that moment as it changed my life. I snapped and tore out of bed, yelling as loud as I could, and got into his face. He backed up and I moved and started to chase him. I was out of my mind with revenge. It was all coming out at one time. I chased him around and around. I finally went outside and called him out. I told him I was going to kill him. I was screaming and every guy in the shack was in awe, as they knew something big had just happened.

Our relationship changed after that night and we started to hang together. (Crazy eh!). About two weeks later he and I were in a bar in Soest and there were a lot of German guys there that night. They didn't like Canadians. We had a lot more money than they had and often stole their girlfriends. Bill and I stood next to the bar and there was a group of them just behind us. This one guy kept reaching back to put his beer on the bar. He would reach over my shoulder each time and lean on me. I told Bill that I was going to have to do something about it, but he just laughed and said I didn't have it in me. The next time the guy did his number, he made it very obvious that he was doing it on purpose. I looked at Bill, looked back at the guy, reached out with my left hand and grabbed his shirt. I pulled him towards me as hard as I could while my right hand was cocked. My fist came across and nailed him right on the jaw. His body came level at the waist and he crashed to the floor. Play the "Rocky" song now. The place broke into an uproar with all the Germans trying to get at Bill and me. The entrance was down a long hall and Bill and I fought our way out, side by side. We eventually made it out unscathed. We looked at each other and we started to laugh like two drunks. I hit a guy and I liked it. Bill and I became friends for life that night and he is the only guy I keep in regular touch with all these years later.

In the ordnance corps there was three major trades. Mine was clerk accounting, which meant managing the paperwork involved in keeping enough supplies on hand. Another job was as a "store man". A store man handled the supplies when they come in or were being shipped out. He had physical access to all the army supplies and could, if he wanted, help himself to whatever he desired. It was a matter of being able to get the items out of the place unseen. One of the guys had decided he wanted to grab some "thunder flashes". A "thunder flash" was an imitation grenade used for practice on manoeuvres. It looked just like a stick of dynamite and when ignited, sounded like the biggest firecracker you have ever heard. To ignite it you had to remove the top and strike it like a match against the top. You had about a three or four second delay and then KABOOM.

There was a small gasthaus near camp where we all drank. The owner gave us credit, but he was cheating us. Eric was his name and each payday when we would go down to pay, we would find a few more beers on our bill then we had consumed. It was time for a payback, so we decided to blow his bar up with thunder flashes. The day came and three of us got in my Renault, slid the roof back, and headed for Eric's. It sat on the side of a small, narrow one-way cobblestone road. The door was set on the right side of a small entrance way on the right hand side of the road. We cruised by and there was no one outside to see us. We went around again and it was still safe so on the third time we slowed down and as we coasted by my friend tossed two thunder flashes into the doorway. We moved on up the street, around the corner and heard the boom, boom as they blew up. I went back the next week and saw that we hadn't killed anyone or done any permanent damage, but the Germans in there must have had a whole lot of flashbacks. We carried on into Soest and looked for another target. This poor old drunk German who happened to be taking a leak against a fence was our choice. We tossed the flash under his feet and drove off. If there was a way to sober up, this was it. That poor guy either died or quit drinking that night.

Next to our camp there was a glider airfield. We were out in the country surrounded by farms and this airfield. A few of decided that just because we had had a few beers, that was no reason for us to not go over for a ride. We were standing beside the landing area in a matter of minutes. We watched as this motor less plane, looking like a large model, gracefully surrendered its self to gravity and gradually placed itself on the grass, rolling to a stop in less than a hundred feet. As soon as it stopped, it leaned to one side, balancing on the edge of one wing. The canopy popped open to allow the two occupants to step out on the ground. I was the first of our gang to fly. I climbed into the front seat, with the pilot strapped in behind. There was a long cable stretched out about 800 ft or so from the plane to a large gas engine that ran a spool that gathered up the cable causing the plane to gain speed and soar upward. As soon as I was strapped in, that engine roared to life, sucking up that cable like a hungry dog. We were in the air in an instant and rising at about a forty-five degree angle until we reached the point where the cable would start to pull us back down to earth. The pilot released a lever that freed us from the cable. The world went silent in that instant. There was only the wisp of the air as it passed over the plane, no man made corruption of quiet. It was to experience true serenity. As I looked forward I saw our camp with all the H huts lined up in meticulous row after row like lines of dominoes all ready to be pushed over. We made a turn to left searching for an air current to soar upon and then to the right, without success. The pilot guided us back over the field, lining us with the landing strip. He applied the flaps, slowing us down to almost a jogging speed as we gently returned to earth. At the last second he flared the plane and the rear wheel touched the grass with the front coming down a few seconds later. I learned to fly many years later but it was never as memorable as that experience.

I met a guy who headed up the motorcycle club on camp. He had a huge BMW that he let me ride occasionally. He also became my instructor to get my army motorcycle license. He taught me to ride as a dispatch rider. This entailed riding a 1958 Triumph Springer. It was rigid frame with no shocks, only two springs under the seat. It was made more as a road bike than as an off road. We started on the roads and soon progressed to riding up steep embankments, across ravines, and over farmer's ploughed fields. At first, I spent a lot of time on my butt, as the bike and I would tumble back down the hill. Or on my side as a furrow would catch the front wheel and dump me. I was determined to overcome and become a dispatch rider. The trick was, on the hills, to use the torque of the bike, keeping all the power available and clutching your way up the hill as you stood on the pegs and leaned forward over the handle bars. For the plowed fields you had to ride like crazy, again standing on the pegs, only this time having your butt as far back as possible, allowing the front wheel to bounce up and over the furrows, instead of digging in. By going as fast as you could, you could stay on top, riding from one ridge to the next, the same as a downhill skier bounces over moguls. I soon had my license and was tearing up the German roads between camps with documents or packages to deliver. I often would sign out a bike from the motor pool just to go for a ride. They didn't know if I had an order to do so or not.

This same guy who taught me to ride was in the ordnance corps as a tailor. He had access to all the canvass anyone could ever need. It was all in army green khaki color and in a light weight. He came up with the idea to make gun cases to store our rifles in so that they wouldn't get dirty while in our lockers. He made a bunch and asked me to sell them for him. It was a 50/50 split and I sold the first bunch in a day. Every guy had a rifle and this would save having to clean it as often. I forget what we sold them for, but we sold lots. The real score came when we hit the infantry guys. They used their weapons a lot more often than we did and had to clean them every day because they were inspected so often. When I hit their camp with the cases, it was mayhem. I sold so out every time and we pocked a ton of dough.

Another money maker was selling cigarettes and whisky on the black market. We were each issued a ration card and could buy four bottles of booze and four cartons of cigarettes a month. It cost $2.50 for a 40 oz. of Canadian Club while cigs were a dollar a carton. Most guys smoked back then but the few that didn't had their cards available. I would buy them, get the smokes and head downtown where it was a quick sale at five times the money. I would take my little Renault and slide the roof back, pull up behind the bar I was dealing with, and toss the smokes over the fence into the back yard. I would then go inside to get paid. I never was caught but came close when I took a case of liquor into Norway. The border guard wondered what was in the box but didn't look.

I often went alone to the bars and was often successful in meeting the ladies. This one night I was at the Blue Bar in Soest and there was a bunch of Brits drinking it up. In the group was a real pretty redhead and I took a liking to her. The group was made up of daredevil motorcycle riders who toured with a big steel cage in the shape of a ball. It was about twenty-five ft. in diameter and they would get two bikes and start riding all around, up and down, barely missing each other as they did. It was very exciting. I had actually watched them that afternoon with some friends. I was getting along great with the girl and things were looking good. We danced for an hour or so when I was grabbed from behind and tossed to the floor. I was then picked up by three guys and tossed down a flight of stairs. I was smart enough to know it was best to get out of Dodge. I started to jog towards another club where I knew some friends would be. I was going to recruit some help and take care of business.

After twenty minutes a car screeched on its brakes beside me, the doors burst open, and the three guys jump out. No words, just action. There was a railway track right there and I took off down it, but I couldn't out run them. They had me down and I was being punched and kicked. After trying to protect myself I began to realize this was real trouble and I could get killed. Somehow some super strength came and I got up and again took off down the tracks. This time they didn't follow.

Another vacation time had come up so a Canadian civilian, Doug Wilson, who worked in the same office, and I decided we would go to Spain. Our plan was that we would take a train from Soest to Basil, Switzerland and transfer to another train going to Barcelona, Spain. The train was to leave Soest at four am so we decided we would go and have a few beers and then wait for the train in the car. Great idea except we both passed out in the car and awoke at around six am missing our train.

We decided to catch another train to Switzerland and spend the night there so we could make the connection the next day. I had brought along a forty oz. of Canadian Club and after a while in the compartment we shared with a German family, I took out the bottle to ease the hangover. I passed it around and we soon had a party going. No one has ever had so much fun as that family and I did that day. Wilson was too sick to drink and so was sober when we got to Basil. I, on the other hand, was passed out in my seat. When the train arrived, he had to carry out the luggage and then help me out into the station. I was unable to walk and he was at a loss as to how to get us to a hotel until he spotted a luggage wagon with huge wheels that was used to carry luggage from one train to another. He quickly commandeered it, loaded me and our luggage, and headed out to the streets of Basil. I can't remember much about the journey, but I woke up in a room the next morning with a head the size of a watermelon.

Later that day we got on the scheduled train we had missed the day before only twenty four hours late. There was no drinking this day as we traversed France and entered Spain. At the border we were interviewed by soldiers armed with machine guns; very intimidating. Their uniforms were unique and topped with a hat like a round bowl with a large flap standing up in the back. We got through and eventually found a hotel in Barcelona.

The hotel was about a block from the bullring so we went to the bullfight the next day. We bought the cheap seats which turned out to be in the sun. The sun in Spain is bright and strong and I would choose the shade if I ever went again. The event starts with a huge parade of brightly dressed men and several horses all covered in huge pads, much like very thick packing blankets. They come into the stadium, salute the crowd, and leave again. The first of six fights begins with a bull rushing into the arena. He is a magnificent beast, his black coat reflecting the sun. He has a presence of pride as he prances around the ring but has nothing to chase. Then a couple guys on the horses come in and the bull chooses his target. He lowers his head, slowly picks up speed, and heads for the side of the nearest horse and picador. As he charges, the horse moves out of the way giving the picador the perfect chance to stick a three ft. ribbon covered spike into the muscle on the back or neck of the charging bull. This happened over and over until there were about six or seven spears with ribbons flying, hanging from one side of the bull. I was told that this is done after they watched how this particular bull would turn his head to gore his target. They planted these to balance his head turns, making them more straight and predictable. The next dude comes out on another padded horse. This guy carries one large spear and when the bull charges he places the spear on the top of the neck where it cuts the muscle of the bull's neck in a way that the bull can no longer lift his head as high. All this takes around fifteen minutes until the hero of the day struts onto the field to huge applause. He is dressed in pink or lime green or some other gaudy color. He comes in to wave a flag and to tease the bull into insanity. The bull charges and the matador then sweeps the target out of his way. Teasing him over and over again until the bovine is exhausted. His rage is burning out and his speed slows to a walk. Finally, the end comes as the hero decides it is time for the coup de grace. He torments the beast one last time until it is lined up just right. The bull charges into the blade that had been hidden until now. The matador aims for the top of the neck where if he hits the right spot, the blade will quickly slice into the heart and the end will come with the animal lying dead at the hero's feet. All went as planned until the blade missed the heart and entered the lungs. The beast didn't die but continued on into the center of the arena with the sword stuck in his body. Blood was pouring out of the bull's mouth choking him, spilling onto the dirt, with each cough from his mighty lungs producing another bucket full of red. His life was ending. He ran around in confusion until he collapsed and died. There was no cutting of the ears or tail for this matador, only the loud boos from the crowd, accompanied his exit from the arena. A team of horses then came in, chained the carcass, and dragged it into the abyss. This went on all afternoon. Not all as gory, but all with same end as the majestic beast is dragged out – dead.

We met a couple of American girls from Los Angeles who were staying at the same hotel. We spent the next four days together touring the city. The hotel included breakfast and left a bottle of red wine on each table. The four of us came in on the last night and sat at a table for a while. We drank three or four bottles of wine as we partied the night away. The next day Wilson and I headed out to the town of Sieges. We had been told that this was one of the nicest towns along the whole Mediterranean coast. We boarded the train in Barcelona and headed south.

For some unexplainable reason Wilson decided to drink on this forty mile journey. Neither of us claims to be the world's smartest people, but on this holiday we were placing ourselves near the bottom of the pile. He had a twenty six oz bottle of cognac in his pack. He opened it and almost downed it all in a few slurps. The bottle was empty in less than an hour and Wilson was hammered. The train rolls into Sieges and I have to get Wilson out. He was 6'2" and weighed around 250 lbs. I grab him as best as I can. I push, pull, and drag him off the train. It takes a long time, but I eventually get him onto a bench. I turn and jump onto the train to get the luggage. I reach for the first bag and feel a jerk and then another. The train's moving and I'm stuck on it. I look out the window and see Wilson passed out on the bench. The train rolls on for about twenty minutes and comes to a stop at the next station. I get the luggage out and wait another half hour for the next train going back to Sieges. Another twenty minutes and I am back. I unload the luggage before going over to where I had left him, but no him, just an empty bench. I begin to panic; then I see a large crowd gathered at the end of the platform. I approach, pushing people aside, until I find Wilson lying on the ground out cold. One of the bystanders tells me they found him passed out on the tracks and dragged him off before the next train arrived. This is just insane. At least I didn't almost die in Basil.

I found a pension for us to stay. It was a small house in the middle of town. Our room was on the second floor and overlooked the street. We spent the next few days in the bars and on the beach. Much fun was had. On a telephone pole we spotted a poster promoting a local wrestling match to take place the next day. It was a troupe of professional wrestlers who traveled from town to town. Wilson tells me he had been a college wrestler and wants to go to the match.

We spend the day as normal, drinking and partying in the local bars. He was pretty hammered by the time the match was to take place. We got there a little late and stood at the back. A few fights take place with the heroes coming out on top. Wilson starts to get very boisterous and vocal, urging the underdogs on. All of a sudden there is a loud roar in my left ear and I see Wilson as he takes off heading for the ring. This drunken Canadian is running down to a wrestling ring in a small town in Spain. He hits the stairs and bounds into the ring. Heck, he was in better shape than half the wrestlers. He is screaming his head off, swearing at everyone, and trying to get his hands on any wrestler in the ring. He didn't have to wait too long as out from the back of the curtain comes every wrestler in the troupe. They all jump into the ring and put a beating on poor old Wilson like no one has ever experienced before. They toss him up high in the air and watch as he crashes back to earth. They use every hold in the book on this poor, drunk, ragdoll. Wilson is swinging madly and connects a couple times but the end is inevitable as he was tossed up and over the ropes, chased out the back door of the arena. The crowd was going crazy, cheering him as he made his escape. I was at a loss as to what to do. I didn't want to die, at least that night in Spain.

I went out the front door and around to the back to find my friend. He was not as hurt as he could have been, but he wanted to kill someone. I had expected that but I thought he would want revenge on the wrestlers. No way. He was mad at me for not getting in the ring to help him. I'm no genius, but I sure am no dummy and I would not have gotten into that ring for anything. I remember what had happened to the bulls in Barcelona. He wouldn't let go of it and by the time we got back to the room he was beside himself. We got into it and I knew who was going to lose this one. I fought as best as I could but the only thing that saved me was that he was still a little drunk. It ended with him trying to push me out of the second story window. I had my hands hanging on one side of the window frame and my feet on the other with Wilson pushing in my middle. I was screaming as the owner came in and saved my butt. We were given the boot from the home and headed back to Germany the next day.

We got home safely from the death defying trip of Wilson inspired insanity. Soon after I found out that as Canadian soldiers, we were allowed to purchase new cars without any tax or duty and that the government would pay for the shipping when we went home. I started to look around and decided I wanted an MG midget. A telephone call home arranged the financing.

A brand new, fire engine red one cost 1800 Canadian dollars, delivered from England. I was now the guy the officers were talking about when they held their safety talks about driving in Germany. The day after it arrived, the whole unit was lined up and the major might as well have said

Metherel we think you'll kill yourself with that car. Close, but that didn't happen.

A couple of weeks later I joined the car rally club in camp and found another way to spend some weekends. We would meet at a predetermined starting point, given a description of the route we were to travel and where we were to end up. We would then try to find our way around different country roads, going at high speeds with stops to locate certain landmarks. We needed to describe the landmarks to prove we had been there and had followed the right route. About twenty cars were driven by crazy Canucks with co-pilots whose jobs were to read the directions. My new friend Kalenchuck and I had a blast, especially at the parties at the end of each rally. I have always liked speed, even now as a senior citizen, but as a twenty year old kid, I was nuts. I drove that MG like Sterling Moss at Sebring. It would corner on a dime, holding the road like glue. I would look over at Kalenchuck as he turned blue and add a little pressure to the gas pedal. We won some but lost more because I would be ahead of the time allotted. You were to take a specific time to go between each checkpoint and I didn't slow to the correct speed.

The weekends in Amsterdam increased with the new wheels. On one momentous occasion, I was drinking in one of the favorite bars when a very pretty girl came in looking a little lost. I smiled and she smiled back. We had a few drinks and she let it be known that she was interested in a more intimate time. We found a hotel and after a few hours I drove her home. We kissed goodbye outside the car and I drove away. I thought that was nice and over - OH, NO! NO! NO! - The next night I was in the same bar when I felt a tap on my shoulder. A real big guy was standing there and asked if I had a red MG. "No, but I would like to have one." I replied. He was looking to beat up and hurt a guy who had a red MG. The guy had been with his wife the night before. He started to talk to me and said that she had found out that he had been down to Canal Street and this was her way to get back at him. I convinced my "new friend" that I just looked like the guy with the MG and I sure hoped he could find him. Another life saved, how many did I have left.

One time a guy and I were driving on a highway at night near Dortmund. It was in winter and was raining as hard as possible. I guess we entered into a cold front and in less than a second all the rain on the windshield froze. The windshield was covered with about a quarter inch of ice with the MG going about 100 kilometers per hour - PANIC CITY! - I rolled down the window, stuck my head into the rain, and somehow got the car to the side of the road.

In our camp in Soest, the single soldiers lived in barracks that were referred to as shacks. Our shack was in the shape of the letter H with about twenty guys living in each section. The washrooms and showers were located in the middle. We only had about sixty guys in our shack, so we used one section as a community living area with sofas, a TV, and a bar. We had card tables and a beer machine that worked just like a pop machine at home. One mark (twenty five cents Canadian) and you had an ice cold German beer in your hand. Like all young single guys our lives were focused on sex and booze with a little work during the day.

Some of the guys had been in the army for many years and were alcoholics. My bed was next to one of these guys. Slicky Walsh was about forty-five and still a private. I had the bed next to him for about four months and I didn't know he was on the wagon or even drank. One night Slicky fell off the wagon and got so hammered he passed out. I was away from the shack until late and didn't know about it, going to bed as normal. At about two am this quiet guy went wild and was completely crazy. I woke when he started screaming. He was lifting one end of his bed six feet off the floor with one hand. He was trying to kill something only he could see with the other. He had the full blown DT's. This went on for ten or fifteen minutes until he crashed to the floor. We put him back to bed. Slicky was never the same again and sent back to Canada soon after.

Another night a couple of the guys got hammered in the shack. They decided they were hungry for chicken. In their wisdom they thought it would be smart to get a chicken from the farm just outside the south side of camp. So off they go, sneaking out under the fence, and get into the farmer's chicken coup. They steal a chicken, kill it, and crawl back into camp. When the rest of us woke up the next morning we found the two guys passed out in two lounge chairs. There were feathers all over the room, chicken guts on the floor, and a hot plate left on with pieces of this fowl burned black and stinking. The best part was the raw chicken leg each guy had in their hands and the blood and crap all over their faces. Somehow they survived.

Another guy passed out one night and was so drunk that he didn't wake up as we carried him out to the parade square, bed and all. Imagine how he felt when the Sgt. Major found him that morning. He is probably still running around that square.

It came to Christmas of 1967 and a plane had been chartered for those who wanted to go home for two weeks. I paid the fare and landed in Montreal and took a bus to Peterborough. I had a sister born in 1965, so I spent a lot of time getting to know her. I don't remember much else except one night after I had gone to the bar with a friend I came home hammered and tried to call my Dad out. I had a lot of pent up anger but he was smart enough to get me calmed down and into bed to sleep it off.

When it was time to return to Germany, I headed back to Montreal to catch my flight. I was in town a day early so I stayed at the barracks. I bumped into a guy who had been my senior. We spent some time together and at one point he pulled out some pot. I had never smoked it before. This was to be a part of my life for the next fifteen years. I sure enjoyed the high and the tranquil feeling it gave. I bought a few joints to take back to Germany with me.

I was lucky that I cleared German customs. I shared the weed with a couple of other guys and soon was out of stock, without a source for more. The next weekend I headed for Amsterdam where I knew it would be available, but I had no idea for how much. I got into my hotel and headed out to score the dope. I soon met a guy standing in a doorway who offered to sell me a large bag. I bought it and hurried back to my room to get high. I quickly rolled a fat joint and lit up. I didn't feel much after the first joint so I lit a second. The guy had sold me bag of oregano.

A big lesson but I soon found the real thing. I didn't use it as much as I drank, but it was always at hand.

I was usually hanging out at the same four or five bars in Amsterdam and becoming friends with the bartenders. The working girls, who didn't work in the windows, often plied their trade in these same bars and I got to know many as quasi friends and not just as a customer.

There was a girl who I got kind of close to and actually had feelings for. It was a sort of an Irma la Douce type relationship. Pretty hard to be jealous with a girl who makes her living sleeping with several guys, but we were friends. Whenever I would walk into the bar she would buy my beer and we would plan on spending the night together. It sure gave me some status with the other guys. Crazy when I think of it now. I took her to the movies one afternoon. We saw Dustin Hoffman in "THE GRADUATE", having a great time. I'm sure it was the first time she had been treated with any kind of respect. Later that night we wanted to be together, but if I stayed at her room, I would have to pay the all night fee to whoever ran the house. I didn't have that much money so we snuck off to another hotel. All was well until morning when we were awoken by heavy banging on the door. I don't know who they were, but four big guys came in and took her away. They left me alone. I don't know if they were police or if she was "owned" by gangsters. I never got to see her again. I suspect that she knew she would be in trouble for what we did and she was willing to face the consequences. I really did like her.

The only other girl I cared about in those days was married to a good friend of mine. He was from Quebec and was raised in an orphanage by some priests. He never told me about that, but a mutual acquaintance told me years later that he had a tough upbringing and suffered all kinds of abuse from an early age. We served together and he encouraged the relationship with his wife. She and I would spend hours together. I must of had some moral values as I knew I could sleep with her whenever I wanted, but I didn't. This went on until I left Germany. I am sure that his abuse led to some kind of inferiority problem and he felt he deserved to lose her or he felt inadequate. I am not a shrink, but this was screwed up.

The feelings we had for each other were real and could have made for a real mess.

Another holiday time arrived and one of the chicken killers and I headed out for Spain. We packed the MG with a couple suitcases strapped on the rack on the trunk and a 24 of 'Snap-Caps' (German beer in a bottle with a porcelain reusable top) under his feet.

All went well until late the first night when we were going around the mountains in Switzerland. We were drinking a few beers and were in a hurry to get somewhere. We got behind a truck and it was impossible to pass. There was no other traffic on this narrow mountain road but time was passing slowly. We were getting tipsy and tired. I decided to end this and pulled out to pass the truck. I got about halfway past him when another truck appeared from around a hidden corner, heading right at us. We were dead men. I don't know how but by some miracle we ended up in front of the first truck. It was all over and somehow we made it. About thirty years later I made contact with chicken man. His first words to me were, "How did we survive that"? I can only think that another angel made an appearance. "Thank you Jesus".

Soon after we returned to camp we learned that our OFP (Ordnance Field Park) was going to be closed. We were given six months warning. I had been in the army for almost four years by then and was going to be eligible for a promotion. To be promoted you needed to be twenty years old and have passed a junior NCO course. If I changed units, I would lose any seniority I had and the guys in my new unit who were in similar situations would get to take the course before me. I talked to one of our officers and he agreed and told me that I would be in the next course.

Of course I wanted to celebrate the only way I knew how. I went partying with some friends, met a dolly and woke the next day at about eight am in an apt in downtown Soest. I was in big crap as I was to suppose to be at work for check-in parade at eight. I grabbed my clothes and jumped into the car, drove straight for camp, into the unit yard where I saw the sergeant and told him I was here. I was in for it and got ten nights of extra duties. Had I been sharper, I would have gone to the shack, got my uniform on, and just went to my desk. I didn't know it but during roll call a friend had covered for me by yelling "here" when my name was called. - Darn it!

I left for the course ten days later. It was a six week course designed to sort out the future leaders from the lifelong privates. It was very physical with lots of parade work, hours of classroom training, and a thirty mile march at the end. Lots of guys dropped out during an exercise designed for each guy to lead the squad by guiding with a compass, to a specific location. It began about five pm, and was more difficult in some locations. I got one of the worst. It was about eleven pm, no moon, and we were all exhausted by then. My name was called and I was handed the compass and given a direction. It was straight up the side of a heavily treed valley wall with at least a forty to fifty degree climb. I said, "Ok guys, here we go." and headed up. It was hell. We were all wearing huge packs and some guys just couldn't make the climb. There was a lot of bitching going on and I was told that I must be going in the wrong direction, but each time I would read the compass, it showed the same way, straight up. It was hard to keep the guys together and have them follow me when some thought I was going the wrong way. I kept going, eventually I making it to the top. We came out onto a plowed field. Off in the distance I saw a lantern, the destination. I made it. I would have failed the course if I hadn't.

We were all taught how to instruct on military manoeuvres, parade square marching, and classroom work. We would give classes on how certain guns worked. I excelled at it. For some reason, I loved to study what I was to teach and was able to get the info across to the guys each time. I scored the highest grades in my squad in classroom work and did real well on the parade square drills. I was down a little on my leadership marks, but scored high enough to get a good overall mark. I had matured a lot since the apprentices.

During our final two days we were on overnight exercises with a mock attack on an enemy. We marched for hours and surrounded their camp. We snuck up, avoiding their sentries and then we charged. Guns were blazing with blanks and thunder flashes were being tossed in every direction. I ran straight into their camp but on the way I ran into a tree branch, which damaged my left eye. It was bleeding a little and it started to swell up. I didn't say anything, but a couple guys saw it and told the sergeant. We all moved into a wooded area, dug trenches, and crashed for the night. I woke up about three hours later with a sergeant calling my name. He had a medic look at my eye. The medic said I had to go to the hospital to be checked out. I said I didn't want to go as it didn't hurt very much and I had to complete the march the next day to pass the course. The sergeant came over and said that it was okay and I didn't have to do the march. It was a long hard march and a few guys fell out during it. I got to ride the whole distance.

Graduation was the next day and an officer from my unit was there. He came to present me with my corporal stripes. That meant that I was the first guy promoted in the whole course. Go figure. For a while afterwards, I was the youngest corporal in the Canadian Army. I am sure a younger guy was promoted in the next week or so to take the honor from me.

4 OFP was disbanded soon after and we were all sent to different units. I was posted to a unit in Iserlohn, a small town about fifty km to the west of Soest. It was to be my last year in the army and I must admit I slacked off quite a bit. I wormed my way into being the dispatch rider at the new posting, much to the frustration of my Sgt. He saw through my ways and had it in for me, but I was able to keep one step in front of him. My job was to insure that a specific truck was loaded with several different supplies like flashlights, Coleman lanterns, etc. I had really lost interest in military life and didn't do the job as well as I could have. I was always out on the motorcycle going from one camp to the next. The officers seemed to think it was slick to have their mail, etc. moved by dispatch and I was always able to find a reason to sign out a bike.

One day we all received a notice saying that HQ was looking for about thirty soldiers to be trained in winter combat. The soldiers chosen were to be taken to the Alps in southern Germany for a weeklong skiing course. I, and every guy in camp, put our names in and somehow I was among those selected. The day to travel arrived and we boarded the bus for a short trip to the train station in Dortmond. Most of the guys had packed a couple bottles in their pack. Remember the trip to Spain? This time I didn't imbibe, but a whole lot of other guys did and so by the time the twenty hour trip was over there were Canadian soldiers passed out all over the train. We pulled into the station and were all loaded into a bus for a trip going thirty miles up to the ski village. We went up and up and up this mountain road with drops of thousands of feet just outside the windows. It was the scariest ride in my life. I could not understand how a bus this size could maneuver up the steep narrow road. It took about two hours to reach Garmisch. It is one of the premier ski resorts in Germany with beautiful ski villas all around. We all were so excited about our prospects about the coming few days - Skiing, Ski bunnies, Beer, Ski bunnies Bars!...Oh Ya!...Let's party!

The first stop, after we got off the bus, was the ski rental joint. We were each fitted for boots, skis, and poles. They put them on us and when we saw they fit, we started to take them off until the officer in charge told us to each ski over towards him, about fifty ft. away – SKI !!! - Most of us couldn't even stand up without falling, plus we all had heavy backpacks strapped on our backs.

They then shattered all our visions by telling us there was "no way in hell" that they were going let thirty Canadian soldiers loose in that town. We were to be housed in a chalet on the top of the mountain, as far from the public as possible. We were led to a small section of snow where a T-bar lift was working. Out of the thirty, maybe ten even knew what it was, and perhaps five had ever used one before.

One instructor demonstrated how to get on and off the lift. They did not take into the equation the fact that we had very little sleep, most had hangovers, and a few guys were still drunk. The first two guys got on the track with the bar behind their butts and off they went. The first 100 yards or so was on level ground and there were tracks for each ski to follow so it should have been a piece of cake. There were about ten sets of guys on the track when the first two guys reach the part of the track that goes steeper and steeper on the way to the top of the mountain.

The first two guys got in trouble when one of them lost his balance about 500 ft up the hill. As he fell off he grabbed the bar with his hands. He was hanging on to the bar with his skis dragging behind him. His skis wrecked the tracks that we all were to use as he was dragged up the hill. If one guy on one side fell, it caused his partner to fall as it became impossible to remain balanced. So when the dragger let go it caused the other guy to fall off the other side. As soon as the next set of guys hit the wrecked track, the scene repeated itself as they fell off causing even more damage to the track. This play soon became insane as pair after pair of soldiers fell off the lift. In a matter of minutes all of the guys were off. We didn't know how to ski and we were stranded on the mountain in ten ft. deep snow with skis strapped to our feet. We could not get back on the lift as it was moving, so the only way out was to ski down and start over. The guys were skiing in every direction, with some falling every two or three seconds while others were running into skiers all over the ski hill. Some were ramming into trees and bushes, fighting to stand up only to fall flat on their face time and time again. The air was filled with much English cursing, expressing our distress. A few tried taking off their skis to walk down, but that didn't work either because the snow was too deep. What a mess. It soon got worse when the officers who had gone up to the top realize something was wrong; skied down and saw the mayhem. They started yelling, but that didn't help as it just created more madness. Finally the ski patrol arrived. They asked what was going on and who was in charge. We all pointed to the officers, who pointed to the NCO's who were going out of their mind, with no idea of how to solve this mayhem. Someone finally stopped the ski lift allowing some guys to mount up and get to the top. Everyone else eventually made it to bottom to try again. Everyone was sober by now and in another thirty minutes we all were at the top, settled into our chalet. What a start to the next six days.

They started instruction right away, but they expected too much too soon. After half a day learning how to snow plow, they took us down some harder trails. I couldn't keep up and was chastised and finally after two days they gave up on me. I was set free to ski by myself. It turned out to be the best deal ever as I quickly was able to learn without the pressure. The rest were all skiing in groups of ten and made to stop and start together all day while I was all over the mountain on my own. I almost got into trouble when on one day I was bombing down the hill and saw one of the groups standing in a line on the right side. By now I could really move and the stopping was even better so I did a great sliding stop on one ski, to talk to one of my friends. I threw snow up in a big spray that hit the instructor, not the best thing I have ever done. I got out of there in a hurry before he told me to get into line. By the end of the time I was doing great and could even go down between the moguls. I was doing just that when I heard the loud sound of skis bouncing on ice. Just to my left a girl flashed by going about a 100 km/h and riding on the top of the moguls. If she hit anyone they would be dead. I later learned she was a famous member of the German national ski team.

Finally the last day arrived and we all had to ski down the mountain with our heavy backpacks on. It was a real trial for me because of the weight and I fell time and time again. Needless to say I failed the course, but I had a ball and learned enough to be able to ski when I got out of the army.

Back in camp it came to time to request my discharge. It took another two months to get processed and I really had no responsibilities so I spent a lot of time on a motorcycle. I had to take my car to Antwerp Belgium to be shipped back to Canada. It was shipped six weeks before I flew home so it was waiting for me when I got there. I left for home in June 1969 and got my discharge in Toronto soon after.

I got home a different person than when I had left to join the army those six years before. I had been a naive, sixteen year old kid who was really screwed up about life. I had lacked a lot of social skills and was without any confidence in myself. I was returning as a twenty two year old alcoholic. I had gained confidence but only in how to live in the army. I always had a place to sleep, meals at regular hours and friends who thought like I did. My ideas of life, love and sex were far from the norm.

Sex was a commodity without any commitment. I knew it was going to be different outside the military but I didn't have a clue of how to live as a civilian. I was about to learn and fast.

Chapter Three

Lessons On How To Be Married, Live Single And Mess Up A Family

I went home to Peterborough with my MG and moved back into my room at my parents' house. My father's twin brother Jack worked as a salesman for Simpson Sears in southern Ontario. I always had always thought I would start by working with him. That all went to pot when he died a week later after having a stroke while fishing.

I had started to party with a bunch of guys. We would all meet at this campground by the Otonabee River. I had some money as the army paid me back pay, along with six years of pension. It probably added up to a thousand dollars. I partied for about three weeks.

I would have to get a job so I answered an ad for an Electrolux salesman. I showed up for the meeting with about six other guys. We all sat in a circle and watch as this guy, Angus McLennan, told us all about the best vacuum cleaner in the world and how every house in Canada would soon have one. They sold for about $550 and we got $150 commission for each one sold. I started to believe the guy and after two days he took me out to show me how to make a sale. We rode around awhile and he showed me the potential income if I could sell one to every third or fourth house. He asked if I wanted a piece of pie and coffee so we stopped at this restaurant. After a while Angus strikes up a conversation with the owner of the restaurant. She mentions that she is having a tough time keeping the carpet clean with so much traffic. Angus asks if he could try the Electrolux to see if it would do the job. Heck, that vacuum cleaned the floor like new and we walked out with 550 dollars in cash. I was so motivated I wanted to get out there and sell, so I practiced the presentation until I had it down to perfection.

HELLO - MY NAME IS KEN METHEREL AND I AM WITH ELECTROLUX CANADA.

WE ARE HAVING AN ADVERTISING BLITZ IN YOUR AREA TODAY AND WE WOULD LIKE TO ASK IF WE CAN COME AND DRY CLEAN YOUR CARPET FOR YOU - IT IS ABSOLUTELY FREE - JUST SIT DOWN - HAVE A CUP OF COFFEE AND LEAVE THE REST UP TO ME.

I headed out to conquer the world one door at a time. Once I was in the house it was in my hands. In simple terms I would start to vacuum the carpet over and over. The vacuums were very powerful and would suck up a lot of dirt. Every minute or so I would stop and empty the dirt catching bag, making a pile in front of the lady. She would always react in horror. It was shocking for her to think that her house could be so dirty. I would pile on another bag full and then another until it was all too much for her. I would then look at her and ask if she wanted her family to live in this. If she didn't answer I would gather another bag full. Eventually I would go for the close, making it so simple to buy - "For as little as the cost of a pack of cigarettes (25 cents) per day, you can have the clean house your family deserves." I would give her a little bank in the shape of the vacuum, which just happened to hold a month's payment. The coup de grace was when I would offer to professionally shampoo the carpet. "I just happened to have" an Electrolux carpet shampooer with me, so with one sale in hand I would go for a double by showing how the shampooer would save hundreds of dollars in carpet shampooing fees over the life of the carpet. If I got the double sale, I got an extra 100 dollars. The product really was a quality machine with a great warranty. The sales technique, however, left a lot to be desired. It was difficult to get two machines in the back of my MG, so. I had to lower the roof to make them fit.

I sold two units my first day and brought home $300. My mother was ecstatic for me but for my father it was kind of awkward. He was working in the carpenter department at Outboard Marine and the hot shot kid comes home and makes a week's wages on his first day. I later learned that the restaurant where Angus had taken me was owned by his sister. He stopped and sold a vacuum there with every new guy. Whatever, it worked for me and I made my living for the summer, knocking on doors, and piling up dirt. Angus was very excited about my sales. I soon was the number one producer and he wanted to make sure I would stay. The MG was a problem. I could only work on sunny days. Angus was on my case encouraging me to get another car. He convinced me to get a new one by telling me how I deserved it, playing on my pride. I narrowed my choice to a Dodge Barracuda or a Buick Skylark. They both were about $5,000. I forget what they gave me for the MG, but I drove away in a lime green Buick Skylark convertible with a 350 cu in with a four barrel carb. Fast and sweet. My friends were all drooling.

You would think I would have grown up a little, but it was still party time almost every day. It was only a matter of time until I would crack the car up. That time came in a mere two weeks when four of us were in my weekly motel room (my mother had asked me to move out shortly after I got home - I wonder why?). We were drinking at around two am when we got the idea to go find something to eat. One guy was on a motorcycle while the other three piled into the Buick. The bike laid rubber on the way out of the parking lot and so I took off after him. We soon were doing about eighty mph on a main street in downtown Peterborough. I couldn't catch the bike and I didn't see him or the red light he slowed down for. When I finally saw him, I hit the brakes and started to swerve sideways. I was out of control and still at high speed as I roared towards my biker friend He heard the noise and got out of the way just before I came sliding through the stoplight, smashing into a telephone pole. The pole entered the car at about one foot in front of the windshield on my side and buried itself about two feet into the motor. I was in shock as I realized what had happened I thought I must have killed my friend but then I realized there was no crash before the pole. The guy in the back was under age so he jumped out and ran away. The guy on the bike lived around the corner so he took the bike home, came back, and was our "witness" to the car that had run red light in front of me causing the accident. I don't think the cops believed us, but we got off when my father showed up. He knew them all. I'm sure they did him a favor. Not even a ticket. The car was in the shop for three weeks and was made to look like new. As for me, I must have got a little sense from it but not a lot.

I had decided that I wanted to sell real estate and took the six week course. I had a girlfriend by this time and her parents had an upstairs apartment in their house that I rented. I passed the course with high marks and was now a qualified real estate agent working for Bowes and Cocks Reality. They sent me to the Marmara office, about forty miles to the east of Peterborough. My territory was the little town of Madoc, another ten miles further east. I packed up the car and headed for the little house where I had paid for room and board for a month. The girlfriend was in the past now, so I was on the hunt in my new community. There was one hotel with a bar in the center of town where I soon had my own seat. I was coming back to the house at all hours causing the little old lady to soon give me my money back along with the boot. With nowhere else to live, I moved into the hotel. I had a hot plate and a little fridge. The washroom was down the hall. The best thing was no one cared when I came home.

For the first two weeks I had to learn the ropes around the real estate office. I had my own cubicle, as did the four other guys. I was twenty two years old, one other was thirty or so and the others were in there fifties. There was a manager who was fronted by a secretary/receptionist. Each guy had to take a turn at office duty, meaning that whenever a customer came into the office on your day, you were there to help him. I much preferred spending my days driving around the country roads meeting people. I started to make some sales and was able to get quite a few listings. There was a companywide listing contest and I won it. It didn't mean much because everyone wanted to sell in that area. Finding buyers, that was the hard part. My evenings were spent at the hotel bar.

It was the redneck capital of Eastern Ontario with about half the men missing some of their front teeth. Many had the same last name or were cousins by marriage. I can't prove there was inbreeding but they sure looked a lot alike. They mostly wore bib overalls without shirts and were particularly proud of who had the most grease stains. I would have bet that some of those overalls had never seen a washing machine and could stand up on their own,

There was one family who had a shack just outside of town where they ran a welding shop. One evening at the bar, the two brothers were telling me about how they had built a race car and that they needed a driver. I, of course, mentioned that I had owned a MG and raced in several rallies. They had the car entered for the dirt track races that weekend and asked if I wanted to try driving it – YA, HELL YES! I knew I could drive most anything so I showed up with lots of confidence. They had asked another guy before me so he got the first race. He was doomed when he started the race in first gear and every other car went roaring by him. The second race was mine and I strapped in real tight and pulled the strap on my helmet as hard as I could. We started rolling in the warm up laps. The car was running great when the green flag dropped. I was kind of trapped behind a few cars, but as we spread out I kept up and then all of a sudden there was a gap, so I dove into the space, moving into the front. Heck, I was going to win this thing. As I pulled ahead, I felt the car started to sputter and choke. Then it started to miss, only firing every second or third time. My hillbilly mechanics had forgotten that we were running on a dirt track and had left the air filter off. The carb was swallowing dirt, leaving no room for air. We went home losers, but I knew I could drive that car. They asked if I wanted to drive at the big oval paved track in Trenton on the next weekend. "For sure" I said. They said they were going to make the car even safer. What could be wrong with that idea? Saturday night arrives and we get to Trenton. We will be running amongst all these semi-pro drivers. We unload the car and head out for the first race. We had gotten there late and missed the warm up laps so it was straight into the first race. We follow the pace car at a slow pace for two or three laps and then the pace car pulls off and the green flag drops. I put the pedal to the floor. We were soon all heading down the straight at over eighty mph, slowing down for the first corner I could feel the car didn't want to turn for me. It wanted to keep going straight as I fought the wheel. The right corner dropped down causing the tire to dig dirt as it rolled. I made it through the first half of turn one when it started to slide. The momentum kept me going straight ahead until I hit the wall hard. My racing career ended with a bang. The hillbillies had added hundreds of pounds. of steel piping to the sides and inside car for safety, not realizing that the added weight would stop it from being able to turn. I hit that wall like a tank. I could hear the announcer calling my name as I hung my head in shame. The tow truck pulled me off of the track. I didn't answer their calls anymore.

I was always short of money. One of the other salesmen was named Mac Casselman. Mac was a wealthy fifty year old man who really knew how to make a buck. He had been in the horse business for years, owning and training horses, working from Toronto's Woodbine racetrack. He played the horses every day. As soon as the Toronto paper came out, he would call out my nickname, "Flip! Paper time!" I would get his $5 and head out for the local barbershop where the papers were dropped off. I would hurry back with the paper, keeping the $3 change for beer money for the night. Mac would then spend the next two or three hours picking his horses.

Francis, the barber, was a lifelong friend of Mac's and they were forever playing practical jokes on each other. I got the idea to get Mac good and shared it with Francis. It was to take the race program from a few days before and substitute it for that day's, by just taking the new one out and putting the old one in its place. Francis laughed his head off and I did it too. Poor Mac worked forever on that program. I'm sure he would have made a fortune had it been the right horses, but he didn't have a chance. I must admit that I told him what I did before he made his bets, but he never forgot that I got him. He pulled several on me during my year there.

I was also working in the bar of the hotel to help pay my rent. I got to know all the regulars real well. I even got to list some of their property for sale. The prices were so low in those days. You could buy a small farm with an 800 ft house for around $10,000. Whenever I would sell one of these I would have to work like crazy to find another one for the selling family to move into. One time it was just two families trading homes for the same price. I guess change is just good sometimes.

The hotel was also the home to several road building crews who were working on a new highway just north of town. I got into a bit of a scrap with a couple of these guys over something stupid. I kept out of their way for a few days hoping it would blow over. Just then I got a telegram from Kalenchuck saying he was coming home from Germany, arriving in Trenton the next night. I headed down to get him with the usual case of beer. We had a couple as we headed back to Madoc. After we got back to the hotel we decided we would head for Ottawa where Bill was going to be posted. As I packed my bag I heard some yelling out in the hall. It got louder and I could hear my name being mixed in the cursing. It sounded like an army outside my door. They were yelling that they knew I was in there because my car was outside and I better come out or they were going to break down the door to kick my butt. My room was on the second floor with a window facing the main street. There were no fire escapes so the hotel had put a heavy rope with knots every foot or so in each room. Before you could say a word, Kalenchuck and I had the window open and were on our way down to the street on that rope. We jumped into the car and sped off, Ottawa bound. By the time I got back, life had returned to normal at the hotel without me having to lose any teeth.

Another of the regular patrons was a guy named Charlie Hamilton. Charlie was a single guy in his forties. He was the sales manager for a school yearbook publishing company based in Winnipeg. He told me about the company several times, finally offering me a position to move to Quebec to handle the English school accounts. It was time to move on so I agreed. A new chapter just opened up.

Charlie was not the average patron at the bar. He was well dressed and had an air of money about him. He had grown up in the area (makes me wonder now if he had relatives there) and had run a territory himself. He had recently been given the position of Canadian sales manager with the job description of hiring and training salesmen. He would soon move to the head office in Winnipeg. He showed how this was a big opportunity for me. Most salesmen made it as a career, earning enough to save for retirement. The company paid fifteen percent on all sales and in this territory that amounted to fifteen thousand as it had about $100,000 in annual sales. Each territory was owned by the rep and had to be purchased for five percent of the annual sales of three years so I would have to pay $5,000 per year for the next three years. He told me that I could quickly build a $200,000 territory. The company backed up their reps with a draw against commission. In my case there would be a $400 check every Friday. That sold me and I accepted the position.

He gave me some travel money and sent me to Winnipeg for the Canadian sales conference. I would meet the other sales reps while learning about the products. After the Winnipeg meetings we all went to Kansas City, MO where the main headquarters was located and had another four days of meetings with all the American reps. This was a legitimate company and all of a sudden I wasn't a twenty two year old kid trying to sell vacant land in the back end of Canada but instead had become the Quebec representative for Inter Collegiate Press Ltd.

After I came home from Kansas City, I stayed with my parents for a couple days before heading out for Montreal. I only had about $100 of the travel money left in my pocket, but they said that they would send me a check as soon as I had an address. I found a place to stay with no down payment when I told them my story and gave them a promise to pay later in the week. I was running out of money fast. I soon didn't have cash for gas or even food. There was a local tailor shop where I met Richard, the owner. I can't remember how it came about, but he fed me sandwiches for the next few days until the check arrived. I got to be good friends with him and his German girlfriend. I bought seven or eight suits from him during the next five years.

After the check arrived, I paid the rent, much to the relief of the landlord, and started to work. I made a lot of sales calls in the first month, mostly to the existing accounts. Charlie called to say he was coming to town. I picked him up at the airport and we headed out for an appointment at one of the schools where we already had an account. The school was on the south shore across this long bridge running out of Montreal. We got about halfway across when the car sputtered and choked itself to death. I had forgotten to fill up with gas. What a great way to impress my new boss. I left him in the car as I hiked across to find gas. I got back in about forty five minutes and found him asleep while cars were racing by with their horns blaring.

We would have rather difficult relationship during the next few years, not because of that experience, but because he would use my draw checks as a weapon to achieve his own goals.

I was doing well, signing new accounts, learning the business. The best part was the colleges and the girls who were the editors of the yearbook. I soon learned I was back in Canada and what worked in Germany didn't make it back home.

I reconnected with some army guys who had got out of the army around the same time as I had. They were all living in the same apt. building in downtown Montreal; one block from the Montreal Forum. There was a guy from Calgary, an actuary working for Sun Life, who had become friends with the guys. He had an apt so I moved in, sharing the rent. I got the hide-a-bed in the living room. I had a great time for the next few months, with lots of parties in one or another of the apts. It was just around the corner from Crescent St., the English party section of town where there were a lot of bars. My favorite was an English pub on St. Catherine's Street. I hung out there and got to make a lot of friends.

One night when Charlie was in town we were looking for seats and joined a couple of older guys in a corner. One was Gump Worsley who had been a goaltender for the Montreal Canadians and several other NHL teams. He lived in a small town just outside Montreal and was in town to visit friends. Gump had a reputation as a heavy drinker and he demonstrated it that night downing beer after beer. He was pretty smashed when he pulled out a pair of scissors from his pocket, reached over, and cut my tie in half. He laughed and laughed. I didn't think it was so funny until later. How many people do you know who have had their tie cut in half by Gump Worsley?

I was in there again a couple of weeks later and there was a table of 4 girls who, as it turned out, all lived together. I got to join them at their table. They were all good looking, but a little brunette caught my eye. The blond next to me was cute and showed interest in me. I got her number. I called a couple days later and we got together. I called another day and asked who wanted to go out that night, hoping the brunette would reply. She didn't and I soon learned that I was off limits to the other girls. Marlene (the blond) and I dated a few times. It was getting near Christmas time when she gave me a wool scarf that she had knitted for me. It was the first time anyone had made me anything (except my parents). It really impressed me. All my relationships had ended long before gift giving time. She went home to Ft Francis, Ontario for Christmas.

I went on a road trip visiting schools in towns on the Quebec/Ontario border, north of Ottawa, before going to Peterborough for Christmas. On the way home I stopped to visit my Aunt Anne (my father's sister who disliked my mother) and Uncle Jack. It was an enjoyable evening near Barrie's Bay. As we ate my aunt began to talk about my upbringing. She talked about how amazing it was that I came out of my childhood as a normal guy. Oh, how little did she know? I was so far from normal, but it really meant something to me that someone knew what it was like for me as a child.

After Christmas I went back to Montreal and Marlene. She was an X-ray tech, making a good living. There was a New Years Eve party in one of the apts. and the whole building was invited. Marlene and I planned to go to the party together. I was hoping it was going to be a real special New Years, but it was not to be. At midnight we were all kissing each other when a cute blond who lived across the hall came in. She searched the room and found me and kissed me a long wonderful kiss with much promise behind it. I passed out later that night with Marlene, but my mind was on the other girl.

A couple of days later I asked the other girl out. We went to the hockey game where I was sure to impress her as I had gone to school with Mickey Redmond, an all-star winger for the Canadians. We sat through the game and afterwards headed for the back entrance, where the players parked their cars. After a few minutes Mickey came out, saw me, and yelled out "Hi Ken!" My chest pushed out for a minute until he yelled again" Hello Cheryl!" He knew her better than I did. She worked in a doctor's office and Mickey was one of the patients. My balloon was busted and we walked back to the apt. never to go out again.

Marlene and I spent a lot of time together and eventually decided to get an apt. in my building. We moved in and life was a lot of fun for a while. One of my friends told me he thought I was nuts if I didn't marry Marlene. She was beautiful, had a career and was in love with me. I wasn't quite into that but when we heard her mother was coming to visit, we decided to go ahead rather than let her family know we were living in sin. She grew up in a very strong Catholic family and it would have been a disaster if they found out our secret.

We gathered all of our friends, arranged for a church nearby, bought rings and I asked Charlie to be my best man, (something I would later regret). My parents couldn't make it, so no relatives were there. We were married on June tenth, 1971.

We soon moved to Dollard des Ormeaux, an English ghetto suburb just west of the city. Marlene was soon pregnant and Scott was born in August of 1972, three days before the Canada - Russia hockey series was to begin. I had always been a crazy hockey fan and this series was going to be over the top. The organizers knew the demand for tickets was going to be ridiculous, so they held a lottery for tickets. I entered by mail, over a 100 times. I won the right to buy tickets on the third row at the Canadian blue line.

My parents came to Montreal to see Scott and so my dad and I could go to the hockey game. History calls it the greatest hockey series ever. When we lost the first game, all Canada was in shock. The Russians had come out on the ice in old worn out uniforms; beat up skates, looking more like a beer league team then a country's best. The game started and Canada scored a couple of quick goals causing my father to say, "I was afraid that was how it was going to be"; was he ever wrong. The Russians came back with a furry, scoring goal after goal, winning game one convincingly. I went into a depression that deepened with second loss in Toronto. It was to last for the next two weeks until Paul Henderson's final goal gave Canada the victory.

I somehow hid my anger for much of my life. It was always there but I was able keep it covered most of the time. On one occasion it showed its head as I was driving my Buick from Montreal to Rosemere, a small town 20 miles north of Montreal. There was a four lane highway and I was bombing along when some guy goes roaring by me. He then slows down and so I pass him. It got going a bit and we started to race. It got a little more serious and then he cut me off. When we got to a red light, I jumped out of my car and headed around the back to confront this idiot. As I got near, the passenger door of his car swung open and this thing unfolded out of the side just like a blow up figure. It grew into a giant. It had to be seven foot tall and about 400 lbs. He was the biggest guy I had ever seen. I went into shock as I raced back to my car, hitting the door locks as I sped off.

On another occasion, I was spending the night in a small town in northern Quebec I was having a few at the local bar. I was the only Englishman in the place. In walked a bunch of French wrestlers who had just finished their local show I got in a discussion with one of them at the bar and in my stupidity told them how fake wrestling was. Tests may say that I have a high IQ, but I am as stupid as a rock sometimes. They took the time to show me just how a lot of the moves are made. (Remember Spain?). I was up and down and pressed to the floor after I was spun on his shoulders. Who says history doesn't repeat itself.

Marlene and I had a rocky relationship by then. I had never even had a girlfriend before, only short time affairs ending after a few dates. I never learned to care for someone else, just my own selfish needs. I had never been accountable to anyone, so no one had ever confronted me about my actions or outbursts. I was not accountable for how I acted or what I said. It just got worse the longer we were together.

Marlene's sister Debbie soon moved into our new apt to look after Scott. She was slightly handicapped, having learning disabilities. She was always depressed and often threatened to commit suicide. It was a daily occurrence that got so bad that I once told her that if she was going to do it to please do it the bathtub so it wouldn't be such a mess. Sometimes I make myself sick thinking of how I have acted and the people I have hurt in my life.

I was on the road a lot travelling around the province. Our home life was difficult especially for Marlene. I acted as if I was still single without any responsibilities. I was often out late in the bars. We never discussed it but we started to have an open marriage. I had several relationships with teachers and one that lasted a little longer with a stewardess from Air Canada.

I was hanging around with some of the Montreal Alouettes football team after meeting one of the players, Rudy Florio, at a teacher's conference in Montreal. He was a second string running back and a representative of a sporting goods supplier. I invited him to the hospitality room I held each year for my customers. He brought the sales manager of the company he worked for and we all got along fine. We started to hang out together, spending a lot of time at the local rugby clubhouse. They were a hard drinking bunch of guys who really knew how to party. I had a great time with them. I met Jules Bonn who went on to be the famous guy who invented speed reading. If I had known then how rich he was to become I would have valued the relationship a little better.

Florio and I would party after every CFL game. He was married with about as much commitment to his marriage as I had for mine. The next year at the teacher's convention, I had about twice as many people sucking down my booze. A lot of people, I didn't know, were coming in all night long. It turned out that Florio had made up cards inviting his customers to my hospitality room. That freeloading SOB was telling them it was his party! I guess I got over that and we partied hard together for the next three years until he got traded to BC.

Scott was only two when Marlene noticed he as having a hard time urinating. We ended up seeing a specialist who diagnosed a problem with his urethras. Most people have two, but he had three and another partial one that was backing up. He was scheduled for surgery a week later. I could not handle the pressure as we sat in the hospital so I went out for a drive. I was so distracted that I had an accident while changing lanes. Thankfully Scott recovered quickly. The doctors told us that it probably happened because of the genes for twins we both carried. Her father and mine were both identical twins.

Around this time another guy and I decided we wanted to be pilots and signed up for lessons. I started ground school learning about navigation, weather systems and radio procedure. I needed to have a total of forty air hours to get my licence. Most of the time was practicing take off and landings but the most fun was when we went away from the airport learning to find emergency landing spots. We would line up a farmer's field, add the flaps and head down. If there was someone in the field, they would have their eyes wide open as we buzzed the ground before heading off to another field. The scariest part was learning how to pull out of stalls. We would point the nose straight up and fly until the plane could not keep going up and it would literally fall out of the sky. At the point where it "stalls", you kick in the rudder and let the plane fall to one side or the other until it is face down with the ground in view. When you gain enough speed, you start to flare the plane back to level. It will take the breath out of anyone. The lessons went well and I soon experienced having the chief pilot open the door and jump out during one of my "touch and goes", telling me to keep on going by myself. I applied the power and went around the circuit, lining up for the landing. It was eerie as I looked over at the empty seat on my right for the first time. I reduced the speed, applied the flaps as I nailed the landing. Another tie got to be cut that day. It took me about six months to pass my exams and get enough hours to get my license. I was qualified to fly Cessna 150's and 172's.

I used this to help in the business as I took several yearbook editors up for a ride to get aerial pictures of their schools.

On one occasion, I was flying over north Montreal on a north-south route following a street on which there was a school. I was paying so much attention to lining up the photo that when I looked ahead I was shocked to see that there was a 747 crossing my path about a mile ahead. It was a heart stopper to see this monster aircraft in the air at the same level as I was and I was on a direct path towards it. I quickly turned left and got out of the way of the turbulence that could have flipped us upside-down.

On another occasion, I was on my way into Montreal and the Dorval tower told me to fly on the south shore. I thought that they said on the south side of the island of Montreal. My route put me in the direct path of the takeoff runway. A loud voice came over the radio telling me to lose altitude immediately and to get to the south shore (the other side of the river) I got a total of 100 hours on my logbook before I left Quebec.

I was also racing motorcycles in enduro races (cross country races through forests and dirt trails). I had worked selling bikes on weekends for a Honda dealership and got a smokin' hot deal on a new bike. I would race and Marlene would meet me at the end of the race to take me home. I was totally spoiled and I could come and go as I pleased. I abused this almost every week.

In 1975, our daughter Cindy was born. She was a real cutie. I tried to change my character, giving more commitment to the marriage. I was real hyper most of the time causing people to tell me to slow down and smell the roses. My brain worked at 100 mph with no peace until I smoked pot, got drunk, or fell asleep.

There had been some posters I saw in a school a year before. They said they could teach how to become more relaxed and a more confident person. I followed up and got involved in Transcendental Meditation, taking all the courses. I forget how much it cost, but it wasn't cheap. Through all of it, there was no mention of a spiritual connection, so when the day came to graduate we were all in for a big shock. We were told to bring a new handkerchief, some fruit, and flowers. We each took a turn going into this room and coming out another door into another room. When my turn came I was led into this darkened room where a photo of some East

Indian dude was set up with a light on it. The room was full of flowers and I was told to get on my knees and bow to the picture. I told them I wasn't bowing to anybody, let alone a picture. They didn't know what to do so they told me my mantra anyway (a secret word used to help you focus when you meditated) and let me out of the room. I practiced T.M. for a few months and I have to admit it calmed me down. It really does work. You enter into another realm and your breathing slows. However, the end result was it opened a door into the occult and some strange things started to happen in the house. It was magnified when I would smoke marijuana or hash. A real stupid combination, drugs mixed with the occult.

One time Marlene and I were sitting at the kitchen table with a deck of cards and for some reason I turned them upside down and began picking up a card, one at a time. I then, without looking, began telling her what each card was. I went through the whole deck and was able to tell her the right number and the right suit of every card. It freaked us out.

Some other stuff happened when some friends were over. We smoked dope and started to play with an Ouija board. We read the rules and started to ask questions and that thing moved around telling answers that no one in the world knew except Marlene and me. It was very scary and so obvious that there is a supernatural world; I didn't want anything to do with it again.

It was no wonder the marriage wasn't getting any better with the two of us arguing all the time, messing with the occult and I was using dope. There was to be no peace in the Metherel house.

I was searching for something in life. I never seemed to be satisfied, always feeling empty. What I wanted and thought I needed was to have people tell me how good I was. I could sell just about anything so my self-confidence came from closing sales. I would receive immediate feedback in the form of affirmation and money. I don't think I worshiped the money. I never was one to have a big roll of bills in my pocket. I only wanted to be valued for my success. I was confident in sales situations but not so much in social contexts. I was always ON and tried to sell myself so that people would like me. If someone was to criticize me about anything, I would get depressed. I would then drink/smoke pot to feel better. What a great way to live. I should have worn a T-shirt that said "WILL WORK FOR PRAISE".

I was very successful at the yearbook business increasing my sales by about a $100,000 every year. We had bought a house in Dollard des Ormeau, a new 1975 Ford Thunderbird, and I wore several of the brightest/ loudest suits you have ever seen.

This was long before cell phones had been invented. We all carried pagers so the office could let us know we needed to call in. It was such a pain to have a pocket full of change and to always be looking for payphones. I knew I had to find a better way. Voila! - there was a Montreal company that had a system for mobile communication based on the same radio waves that taxicabs used. It was a huge, heavy unit that fit in the trunk with a large antenna sticking out. Inside the car, on the floor between the seats you had an actual telephone mounted to the floor. There was a rotary dial that had ten numbers on it. To make a call you turned the dial until you found an open line, you then squeezed a button on the headset to reach an operator. In all of Montreal there were only ten lines available. You tell the operator the number you wanted to call and talk away when connected. You had to use caution because the lines were open to anyone else with the phone system to listen in on.

I believed that much of my sales success was due to the absolute commitment I made to motivational tapes. I first heard about them from a friend who had an office next to mine in downtown Montreal. He was doing great in the insurance business. I started to listen to some of his tapes from J Douglas Edwards about making calls, closing a sale, and overcoming objections. I also listened to Zig Ziglar who was into motivation, telling you how to believe in yourself, and how nothing was impossible…"If you can see it, you can make it happen." I spent hours in my car and I used that time to play these tapes over and over. They became my mantra.

There was another guy who worked for IBM using the tapes. The three of us got together and decided we would hire both Edwards and Ziglar to come to Montreal for a one-day seminar. The tapes meant so much to us that we thought it would be easy to sell out a seminar featuring these two. We had to pay Edwards $1000 and Ziglar $750 for the day plus all their expenses. We sold tickets as best we could but because we were so busy we soon realized we had “bit off more than we could chew.” We looked pretty dumb because we couldn’t sell tickets teaching you how to sell. We had sold around sixty tickets or so at $99 each and were close to breaking even (we had to rent rooms at a downtown hotel, pay for meals, airfares, ads, etc.). When we were three days away from the event the ticket sales went dead. We needed to have an audience so I called some English radio stations and gave them tickets to give away every hour. It got the message out and we had over 100 people attend.

I had to pick up Edwards from the airport when he came in from Arizona. I waited with several hundred people as people came out of the luggage area. Soon a very distinguished looking man walks directly up to me and says, “HELLO KEN!” I was taken by surprise because he could not have known what I looked like. I guess it had something to do with the red and white checkered suit I was wearing. Remember this was in 1975 and bright suits with platform shoes were the fashion.

The seminar was a not a financial success but we got lots of great feedback. We all took in the message, be all that you can be, no mountain is too high to climb, the only limit is yourself, be all that you can be etc. It was an awesome time and everyone walks out on cloud nine ready to take on the world. On the business side we had a net loss of about $1000. The insurance guy and I covered it as the IBM dude bailed, leaving us stranded.

I got to know a lot of people in the high schools. In Quebec there were two school boards; one Catholic and one Protestant. I made friends with a vice principal at one of the Catholic schools. There were several businesses selling to schools for different services and products. One of the most popular services was the fundraising business. All schools were short of money and there was always a need for different clubs or sports. The most popular method was selling chocolate bars with the most successful company in that business being World’s Finest Chocolates. Their rep was a guy named John Laliberte. He was real cocky about how much money he made and he got under a certain vice principal's skin. The vice principal's wife had relatives in the grocery business so he decided to use the contacts and go into the fundraising business. He asked me to be his rep. It was easy to handle different lines when I called on a school. The schools actually preferred to deal with one rep that they knew and trusted. We did well together, especially in the Catholic schools where he had a lot of contacts. He and I worked together for the next four years, making each other a lot of money.

The fund raising business was very profitable and Charlie decided he wanted in. He formed a company and tried to make each of the Inter Collegiate Press reps sell his products. This was outside of ICP and because he was the sales manager and a salaried employee, it was not kosher. Most of the reps had their own line, as I did, and didn't want to sell for Charlie. He made it difficult for anyone who didn't sell for him, especially when we would want an increase in our weekly draw. I never did sell for him and our relationship became worse than it had been before. Charlie was finally let go by Inter Collegiate Press but not before he did a lot of harm to most of the young guys, myself included. He liked all of our wives a little too much and in some cases way too much.

I had other businesses running at the same time. I would hear of needs in the schools and whenever possible try to find a profitable way to meet it. The first was trophies. At year-end, each school would present its annual awards. I found a supplier where I could buy the different parts to build the trophies. They produced a catalogue showing all the different types of trophies, on which we printed our name and tel. number. We called ourselves, "THE TROPHY MAN". I bought a Hermes engraving machine and hired a lady from across the street to run the business. Judy did a great job and eventually bought the business from me.

The best deal I set up was for badges. In those days most schools had winter carnivals. They had badges made with winter designs and the name of their carnival. I found a supplier called E C FORD in a suburb of Montreal and sold to a few schools the first year. It paid 100% profit so I wanted to make it grow. And boy did it grow! We became the number one supplier of badges to schools across Canada in two years. We made a simple brochure using the name ECONOMICAL BADGES with a selection of designs that the company already had on hand. We sent this brochure to every high school in Canada. The school had to send a 50% deposit with every order, which I used to pay FORD. They would produce the badges and I would simply box them up and send an invoice for the balance. I hired another lady to run the mail order business as well as be my secretary.

During my time in Quebec the separatist movement was taking shape led by Rene Levesque and the party he formed called the Parti Quebecois. He was a very charismatic French fanatic who truly believed that Quebec should separate from Canada. He made it clear that if they were ever to take power they would eliminate English from the province.

In the fall of 1976 it happened. They won the election and took power in Quebec. My world blew up in one day. It was inevitable that they were going to close the English schools. No schools, no business. The day after the election I submitted my resignation to ICP. We had sold the house a few months before and had some money saved. We also had bought a Holiday Rambler travel trailer. I took the T-bird to Peterborough and traded it in on an International Harvester four wheel drive wagon. I sold the other businesses to my employees and got out of town. We decided we would go to Florida for a few months and come back in the spring to see where we wanted to live.

We decided to go to Marlene's home in Fort Frances for Christmas before heading south. We packed the Holiday Rambler with all we owned, filled the wallet with about 5,000 bucks, and headed out. All was well as Marlene and I shared the driving until early in the morning, while I was asleep in the back, Marlene hit black ice coming over the crest of a hill. We slide down the hill sideways into the guardrail on the other side of the road. No one was hurt but the damage was appraised at $4,000, all isolated to the back corner of the trailer. We had insurance to cover it all. We drove on to Ft Frances to spend the next week. There was no one able to repair the trailer in Ft Francis so the insurance company told us to get it done in Florida.

We had a great time with Marlene's family over the holidays. Her father and brothers were all outdoorsmen and took the time to teach me how to ice fish and ride Skidoos while I showed them how to drink. They didn't need much instruction and we had a great time. I don't know why they put up with me. I was such an idiot with a big mouth, a real know it all. Her father was in a lot of pain from an industrial accident. He almost lost his thumb, which meant he couldn't work. He was having trouble with the insurance company and he was getting depressed. He took me aside one day to confront me on my insane behavior, especially boozing and running around in a small town. He was a real gentleman. I wasn't.

We got on the road again, heading south. The border guards looked us over as we told them how long we were going south for, wanting to see the cash, et al. It took a few days until we started to hit the sunshine. We first went to the north of Florida but knew we had to keep going when it started to snow. My grandparents were snowbirds on the west side near Tampa, so we headed toward that area. We found a place to repair the trailer. They could do it cheap enough that we could get an awning at no cost.

By the time we got to the Miami area we were ready to settle down for a while. We ended up in a campground in Key Largo. It was a paradise with nice big grassy lots; an "in ground" fenced pool, lots of shade trees, and paved roads. We were having a great time so we decided to stay for a month.

The first weekend I headed off for Ft Lauderdale where there was one of the biggest flea markets in the country. There was this massive field with 1000's of stalls with everything you could imagine. I found the perfect item for us to sell. It was silver jewelry made in the Bahamas. It was selling for $5 apiece retail, but the guy was the importer and wanted to sell wholesale. I bought hundreds of necklaces with turquoise, sharks teeth, puka shells, and mother of pearl all for a dollar or two each. I took it all back to the campground. As soon as I showed it around, it started to sell like mad. Everybody was buying multiple items and I had paid for the whole load in a few hours. This was the best product to sell ever.

Super profit and it all fit in a briefcase. One day we sat around the pool while Scott went from table to table with samples. This was one of the best times we were to have in the marriage. Each weekend I would go to Ft Lauderdale on Friday, buy more stock, set up at another end of the market, and go home on Sunday night. We booked into the campground longer and stayed until it was time to head to Myrtle Beach, where we were to meet some friends from Montreal for spring break. I loaded up with as much jewelry as I could afford before we left.

We found a campground just north of Myrtle Beach and settled down for the next two weeks. There was a candy store in the middle of town with a machine twisting saltwater taffy in the window. But what really attracted me was the small kiosk next to the store. I talked to the owner and made a deal to rent it for spring break for 25% commission. I started doing great business and paid the guy exactly what I owed him each day. He liked me, but I think that he liked the tax-free cash more. I would sleep in the kiosk because there was no security and I didn't want to have to pack it all up at ten pm each night. I just slept in a cot and used the washroom in the store. I also got to party each night in Myrtle Beach, one crazy town at spring break.

After the two weeks we made our way north, stopping at little communities where they were having spring fairs. We would set up the jewelry on tables outside the trailer and then in a day or two, move to the next fair. We stopped in Washington DC, before we finally got back to Canada in late May of 77. We headed for Peterborough where we set up camp at a public campground along the Trent canal, just under the world famous lift locks. Marlene and the kids stayed there for a week or so, while I went to Toronto and sold the jewelry in the front of a department store.

Ft Frances was the end of the journey. When we arrived in mid June, I didn't know what I was going to do for a living. I did an audition for the radio station but without success. After a couple of weeks I had to do something so I headed back to Myrtle Beach for the summer. I needed more stock by then so I called the supplier with the idea I would meet him halfway between MB and Ft Lauderdale.

I got to Myrtle Beach, signed up for the kiosk again, and hired a kid to run it. I then found another location and then another and soon I had a dozen little stores working for me. I was paying my rents and the guys who owned the kiosks all wanted me in them.

All was going great for about two weeks. I was working one location on the boardwalk when a kid walks up and tells me that the shark's tooth he had bought wasn't real. They were real. Sharks shed their teeth often and there are millions available in the Caribbean. Anyway, he accuses me of cheating him and I wasn't thinking so I began to argue with him. If I had had a brain, I would have given him his money back and offer him any other piece that he wanted. We begin to scuffle and he takes off. Awhile later a cop shows up and I am arrested. I go to the can where the police chief goes nuts on me. He is the kid's father. Smart move Metherel. The cop tells me I have a court date in a couple days. I am let out with a fifty dollar bond and a promise to appear...YA - U - BET... I WILL BE THERE... I PROMISE.

I left jail, closed up every store in a matter of a few hours, and I am on the road home. It takes me twenty four hours non-stop from Myrtle Beach, SC to International Falls, MN. That is exactly 1000 miles. I was angry, tired, and lost in my mind. I didn't have a plan or even an idea of what to do. No job, no home, with a wife and two kids.

It only took two days for war to break out with Marlene. I had to leave again. Back into the states I ran. I sold whatever jewelry I had left in Bismark, ND and headed for my friend Kalenchuck's in Edmonton.

Bill had got out of the army in the early 1970's after marrying his flame Linda. I had met her couple of times. She knew I could be trouble so she was worried when I moved into their basement. Bill had opened a large restaurant called Uncle Bill's. He served Ukrainian food. It was fabulous and successful. Bill still liked to gamble and was playing the horses. I'm sure he had some success but lost more than he won. My vices were booze and women, as I had not gambled much since army days. Linda put up with me for a while but I soon was sharing an apartment with Bill's brother Steven in a downtown high-rise. Bill had a concession at Klondike

Days (the annual fair in Northern Alberta) selling perogies and kielbasa. I helped out for the two weeks as Bill pulled in a ton of money. There was a booth next to us with a famous car. To promote their show they played "Little Deuce Coup" over and over and over and over again - EIGHTEEN HOURS A DAY – ONE SONG - I HATE THAT SONG! That was the good part. The bad part was that there were horse races on the same grounds. Bill was able to lose much of what he made at the track.

Later in the month we were all partying in the apt. There was a restaurant on the ground floor so Kanlenchuck bet me 100 dollars I wouldn't streak it. There wasn't much I wouldn't do for a100 bucks, so I went down and cased it out. There were two front glass double doors out to the street from the building; one to enter the restaurant and a second one as the entrance to the apartments. At the back of the restaurant, there was an exit into the lobby of the apt. bldg. I determined it was possible, as I had a way in and a way out. Bill was to hold the elevator door open while Steven was at the front door of the apt. bldg.

The three of us are in the elevator, on the way down, I have a towel around my waist and that's it. Ground floor, the door slides open. I drop the towel and head for the back door of the restaurant swing it open and streak through the kitchen and then the restaurant aiming for the glass doors. I scream - "IT'S FOR A BET!" - As I bounce off a couple tables hitting the door at full speed with my hands out to push them open. The door on left swung open, but the one on the right was locked and shattered when my right hand went part way through it. When I realized what had happened I twisted out the door on the left and headed for the front door of the apt. Steven swung it open and followed me into the elevator. Bill was in hysterics when we got to the elevator. I left the elevator with the towel around my middle and went to the apt. to collect my 100 bucks. I still have a scar on my right hand from the broken door.

Later that summer I remember driving around in Edmonton when I heard breaking news that Elvis had died. I guess that is why I always think of Edmonton when I hear an Elvis song. My time in Edmonton came to an end when I called Marlene. She had moved to Winnipeg with the kids and was working at a hospital in the west end. I decided to go back and try to put things together again. I was an idiot, along with being an out of control control-freak. I didn't know it then, but I had a king size anger problem that was buried most of the time. Marlene, unfortunately, had seen lots of it with still more to come.

I arrived back and found Marlene had an apt. near the hospital. She also had a boyfriend who lived in the same apt. bldg. I moved into her apt, sleeping with her from the start. I thought we were going to try to work it out especially for the kids, but she had other ideas. She liked this other guy and I was in the way. I actually sat at the kitchen table one night as she watched a movie with this guy. How I could do that bothers me. I must have felt so much guilt over my actions that I believed I deserved it...AND I DID!

This lasted for a couple of weeks. I had been hired by ICP as a sales trainer (a position they created just for me so I wouldn't join the competition). Marlene found the relationship unworkable. She and I went to a Blue Bomber football game where the boyfriend sat in a few rows behind us. On the way home she tells me I have to move out. I argue with her and then go into a rage like never before. It all comes out and I threaten to smash the car into a telephone pole. She's yelling, I'm crying. It was nuts.

I have to move out that weekend, so I find a cheap furnished apt. in a downtown walk up bldg. I gather my stuff from Marlene's, kiss the kids, and head out. I buy some beer and cry myself to sleep. I only lasted two days until I decide that if the other guy is out of the picture, I can solve this problem. After a few beers I make my way back to the apt. building to have a talk with him. I see his car in the parking lot so I know he is home. Marlene is at work so I stop to see the kids, then make my way down the hall to his apt. I knock on the door - no answer - then again and again. I go back out to the parking lot to see if his car is still there. It's gone. The babysitter tells me that he has gone to pick Marlene up from work.

I see red. That's enough. I can't take it anymore. I head to the hospital where I see his car. I pull behind it, putting my bumper on his, blocking it in so he can't get away. I march into the waiting room where I see him sitting. He sees me and he starts to scream. I come up to him and drop him with a punch to the jaw. He goes down with me beating on him. Marlene comes out screaming and tries to stop me. I look at her and scream - "I LOVE YOU!"- And kick the dude a few more times before running out of the hospital. I am lost in pain and without hope.

I have nowhere to go so I drive blindly for a while until I make my way to my boss's home. He is an American guy with three teenage daughters and a wonderful wife. I knock on the door; he comes out to find me bloody and crying. He takes me in, calms me down until I think I can make it back to my apt. I drive for a couple miles when a cop lights me up. I pull over and he asks me to come out to the front of the police car. He talks with me for a few minutes like he is my friend. We talk about what happened and he seems to understand. Another cop pulls up and then another. My "friend" is no longer a friend. I am pushed to the ground, handcuffed, and shoved into the back of the car. As we make our way to jail, my sanity starts to come back and I ask, "How is the other guy?" They say he was admitted. That is all they know. As we drive they ask what happened and why. After I tell them the story they say they would have done the same thing. It was probably BS, but it made me feel somewhat better.

I am taken into a large holding cell with about ten bunk beds. There are twelve or fourteen guys leaving five empty beds with only springs, no mattresses. I see that a couple guys have two mats and as I move towards a bed a guy jumps up and slides a mattress to me. He tells me that they had heard from the guards what I had done. I had immediate respect in the cell. The world sure is crazy.

Somehow I fall asleep, only waking when I hear someone yelling. I stretch my arms over my head. Reality rushes in as my hands bump into the cold steel bars. I look ahead where there is a row of toilets without seats and no doors on the stalls. It all comes back as to what I had done. I am sick to my stomach and lost. What do I now, how can I ever fix this mess? I have ruined my life! There is no answer to the pain as I pace around and around the cage, eventually telling a guard I am going nuts. He tells me he will see if he can help. He comes back in a few minutes, taking me to a small office and locks me in there. I tell him I need to talk to someone and in a short while a uniformed Sally Ann guy comes in and we start to talk. He didn't preach or condemn me; I was doing enough of that myself. He let me talk and he listened. It meant so much to me to have someone hear me, sharing my fear and pain. After a couple of hours I was released on $500 bail, found my car and headed for the emptiness of that four walled apartment. After an hour or so I called Marlene and apologized. I don't think she heard me.

I went back to work on Monday morning, confiding to the manager what happened after I left his house. He accepted me as I was, encouraged me hang in there. He and his wife were strong Christians but I didn't know it at the time. I am sure they were praying for me. In a couple weeks, I manage to guilt Marlene into getting back together. Why she did it, I will never know but she did and we moved into a large garden suite near the hospital. Boyfriend was out of the picture and we started to live a somewhat normal life. I would work days in the yearbook business while Marlene worked night shifts leaving me to look after the kids.

One night I was flipping channels and stopped on a faith broadcast. I heard the gospel, got convicted, knowing I needed help. I called in. I was hoping to talk to someone like the Sally Ann pastor but the person who answered talked for a minute and then asked how much I wanted to donate. I hung up. We, as a family, actually went to a church service the next Sunday but nothing stuck and we didn't go back.

A couple of weeks later, we got a telephone call from the Montreal police telling us that Debbie had committed suicide by hanging herself. She had stayed behind when we left Montreal because she had found a boyfriend and a job. Life was on an upswing for her so we had had high hopes she would find a place for herself in life. On one sad day she had lost her job as a cleaner and gone back to the apt. she shared with the guy, only to have him say he was breaking up with her. It was too much for her fragile condition. She saw no other way out but to end it all. She must have contemplated it earlier as she had a rope in the apt. I had to go to Montreal to arrange for the body to be returned to Ft Francis. We all went back for the funeral. Her family was devastated. Relatives, friends and neighbor filled the house without stop. True love was displayed as everyone suffered together. It took a lot out of the parents who had worried and prayed over her for years.

Back in Winnipeg I had to face the law for what I had done. I hired a lawyer who explained to me what was going to happen. I went to court where I had to face a judge. My lawyer explained to the judge the sequence of events leading up to me losing control. He had worked a deal with the prosecutor who agreed not to seek jail time. The judge read the charges and asked how I would plead. "Guilty your Honor", I squeaked out. I was convicted of "assault causing bodily harm"; with the judge pronouncing a conditional discharge and a 500 dollar fine. I had to keep the peace for two years and the conviction would be taken off my record. I did and it was.

I was working hard and started to take a sales management night course at the University of Manitoba. It lasted six weeks. I got the highest marks in the class. ICP started to use me as a sales manager and I began to travel all over the country. I didn't like it because I had to be accountable to the general manager. I hated to have to report to anyone. I suppose it was in response to my military life where we lived under the thumb of our superior every day. I had been on my own for over eight years by then.

On one of my trips I was working with the Calgary rep. whose territory included the western portion of British Columbia. We left Calgary, working our way along Hwy 1 stopping at each school we came to. We were on fire signing ever school to a yearbook contract. The difference from our program to the competition was so dramatic; it was like shooting ducks in a swimming pool. After three days I had had enough and wanted to go back to Winnipeg. I was supposed to stay until Friday but I was bored and wanted to have the representative finish the job on his own. When we arrived in Kelowna, I took a flight out. I got back to the office to the dismay of the GM. He wanted to know why I didn't stay. I told him that if the rep couldn't sell those schools he needed to be canned. Over the next weekend the newspapers were filled with the story of an Air Canada plane going down in Cranbrook, B.C. on Friday night. There was a very good chance I would have been on that plane if I had stayed to finish the trip. Someone was watching over me again.

I found out I wasn't cut out to be a sales manager. Just because I could sell didn't equate into being able to pass on that ability to others. I also didn't like having to show up to an office every day at a certain time, so when the B.C. territory opened up, I took it. We moved to White Rock in the spring of 1978.

We traveled cross country in February 1978 after having picked up the Holiday Rambler from Ft Francis. I had received $5000 against the sale of my Montreal territory before we left Winnipeg. ICP had sent me out a month before to BC to see if I liked it. I actually was going to turn it down when I experienced the rain there because Scott was suffering from allergies. I thought the dampness would be a problem but Marlene convinced me that it would be okay to go.

I had found a duplex in White Rock to rent. We liked the city, but the fact that we knew no one started to wear on us and soon the fighting began again.

Not long after arriving I bought a fish and chip truck with a contract with the city of Surrey for the exclusive rights to sell food in Semiahmoo Park. This park was on land leased from the Semiahmoo Indian tribe, located right on the Pacific Ocean, next to the US border. It had a large parking lot, holding hundreds of cars full of the sun worshipers, who came all summer long. I hired a couple of guys to help work it with me. Out of the blue, my brother Hal shows up from Ontario. He had served time in several prisons by then and was a criminal through and through. My parents couldn't handle him as he had stolen everything he could find from their house to buy drugs. They gave him a one-way bus ticket to B.C. and some travel money, basically sending their problem to me. I let him live in our travel trailer that we parked in front of our house. I made the mistake of giving him a job in the fish truck. One day, I went down to the park, when he was supposed to be working, to find the truck wide open and no

Hal. He was off in the park chatting up some girl. I went off on him, chasing him all over the park to put a licking on him. Later that same night, I was sleeping on the couch (Marlene and I were having trouble and it was getting worse) when I heard the patio door slide open. I could see Hal slipping into the house to rob it. I knew there was nothing of value in the kitchen where he was and so I didn't confront him. I would have if he had tried to go upstairs where the kids were. I tossed him out the next day. It made life even more difficult having to deal with his problems when I had so many of my own. He left town ending up living in an Indian reserve north of Vancouver.

There was a family living in the other half of the duplex. The mother asked if I needed help in the truck. It would work perfect because she could drive the truck to the park, do the cooking, sales, et al, and then drive it back home to give me the money each night. It was working ok, but I wasn't making as much profit on the same amount of product. It was all explained one afternoon when I unexpectedly came down to the park. I jumped into the truck and happened to open one of the cupboards. I found a can of money on a shelf in the truck. My neighbor thought she should be paid more so it was a dollar for me and one for her. She kept her share in the tin can. The rest of our time living next to each other was a little strained after I fired her butt. They moved away before the end of the summer. I worked it daily myself until Sept. and then I just worked weekends. Stealing money was something I just didn't understand. I had been caught as a kid and learned a big lesson. I was to be the victim many times in the years to come.

There was an annual sea festival weekend on the beach when everyone in the Vancouver area would visit White Rock. I was making a ton of money. During the festival I would set up in the park itself, on a grassy knoll next to the bandstand. Everyone was smoking pot and getting the munchies, which translated, into a ton of dough for me. I would get high, make money, and enjoy the music all night long. On the Sunday night, a church group would take over. I was usually high by then, just watching them do their thing. I'm sure they thought I was a crazy man and they were probably right. They later became my best friends.

Later that summer I had to go to a sales convention in Kansa City for a week. I had lost my zeal for the yearbook business and knew I was just putting in time. I started back at the yearbook business in Sept. I signed a few accounts, but it was so much more like work then it was in Montreal.

I was to cover the western and northern sections of the Province of BC so I laid out a trip to the north. I took an overnight ferry from Vancouver Island to Prince Rupert, a long way up the coast. I worked the few towns along the northern route heading towards Prince George. I arrived in the town of Houston around four pm. It was too late to make a sales call so I found the local hotel and checked in. I went to my room, smoked a joint, and then left to find a restaurant. Dope always made me hungry and paranoid so when I sat down in this Chinese restaurant, ripped, I was ultra cautious. It seemed like it was unusual for a stranger to be there as everyone was staring at me. Not a good sign. As another guy comes in, he yells to the waiter - "HEY CHINK". I went cold as he said it. He then said it a few more times. Soon another customer refers to him in the same way. Apparently the whole town called him - "CHINK". I guess I was wondering what they were going to call me. I ate as fast as possible, paid my bill, and headed back to the hotel, watching that I was not followed. There was a sign in front of the hotel for the bar, showing an entrance down some stairs. I decided I would have a couple beers and see what was happening. As I entered the darkened room, a voice in the corner yelled out - "HERE COMES TONIGHT'S ENTERTAINMENT" The bar was filled with Indians, with me being the only white guy in the place. I was stoned, paranoid, and now scared. I turned around and left. I went straight to my room and locked the door. I then dragged the dresser against it as double protection. I never went back to Houston again.

Later that fall we saw a house for sale, just around the corner from where we were renting, for $59.000. It was price we could easily afford as we had sold the trailer and had a down payment. The kids were being subjected to our fights on a regular basis. It seemed like we never had a day of peace. I had had a couple flings during this time. There was no love in that house. The kids were experiencing exactly what I had grown up with and probably worse. I had become what I hated, a man who was out of control, filled with anger, and blaming Marlene. We bought the house, living in some kind of truce for a while.

It all came to a head in April of 1979. The kids were having dinner with us at the dining room table when Marlene and I got into a real battle. Words became like daggers as we tried to hurt each other with blow after blow. She hurled a bolt that must have struck me in the heart because I exploded out of the chair, put my hands on the edge of the table and dumped it upside down. I told the crying kids to go to their rooms as their mother and I had it out. Marlene started to beat on me with her fists so I grabbed her by the wrists and pushed her into a chair to hold her. Something caused me to step over an invisible line and I hit her with an elbow. I had never hit a woman in my life. The moment I did it I knew it was all over. I ran out of the house. I can't remember when I came back, but when I did I told her it was over. I moved into the basement that night never to share her bed again.

We did so much harm to each other but even more to those little kids. It has left scars that, all these years later, have not healed. Not for them or for me. I was a terrible father and I knew it. I moved out of the house a few weeks later after I found an apt. in White Rock. We made a separation agreement and I paid child support. We were to divorce two years later.

Chapter Four

Single, Stupid And High

I took a few pieces of furniture and moved into a one bedroom apt. Unlike Winnipeg, I knew there was no going back. It really was over this time. I felt relief that the constant daily strain had ended. Marlene was working as an X-ray tech at Peace Arch Hospital in White Rock. We tried to set up a visitation schedule so I could see the kids. We had bought a small truck along with a new Honda, so we each had a vehicle.

I started to hang out at the local pub that had just opened. While going to garage sales, I had bought an "as new" coin operated foosball table. I made a deal with the owner to set it up in the pub. It was a success and generated my beer money. I had found a pot dealer in town, becoming one of his regulars. I dated a few girls that I met in the bar. I would work the yearbook business during the week and run the fish truck on Fri to Sun. While the truck was set up near the border I met a girl who was doing traffic control. Carol and I hit it off right away. We both smoked pot, liked taking walks on the beach and just hanging out.

I had brought my off road motorcycle from Quebec. I decided to trade it in on a touring bike and so I bought an 850cc Suzuki with fairing and saddlebags. Carol was with me when I picked the bike up. She liked the bike almost as much as I did. We were doing well until she invited me to spend the weekend with her family on Salt Spring Island. Her father was a lawyer and was real well off. Her mother and sisters became my judge and they quickly saw through my veneer. Our relationship ended soon after.

I had a Surrey permit for the chip truck, not White Rock, so I always stayed on the Surrey side. The towns bordered each other. One day in late June, I had the fish truck set up at the main intersection on the border between White Rock and Surrey across the road from Irly Bird lumber. I needed another shelf in the truck to store cups and plates. I didn't have a ruler or any other way to take the measurement so I used one of the plastic forks. It came out that I needed a piece of wood that was two forks wide and four long. I shut the opening to the truck and went across to the lumberyard with the fork in my pocket. It only took a minute to go out to the back where a guy cut me the board. He gave me a bill for the cashier so I went back in to pay it. There was someone paying ahead of me so I waited my turn. The cashier was a short brunette, real cute, with a nice smile. I said hello and gave her the bill. She asked for so much and I reached in my pocket for some money. I dug down only to feel excruciating pain. I had left the fork in pants pocket and now one of the prongs was about a ¼ inch under my nail. I pulled my hand out, holding it up. The fork was standing straight up from my finger. The cashier lost it, laughing like crazy. I wanted to laugh, but it hurt too much. I pulled it out and handed her the cash. We were both laughing by then and I told her to come over for some free fish and chips. I learned her name was Patsi McKay. I was dating Carol at the time so I put her in the back of my mind for the future.

A few days later I was in the pub and Patsi was there sitting with a guy. She said hello and invited me to sit down. I didn't want to intrude, but she introduced the guy as her brother-in-law. We had a drink and enjoyed the time. Later in the week I was playing my foosball game for a beer when she walked by. She invited me to her table in the corner. I came over to sit with her and two other girls. She introduced me to her sisters, Linda and Sharon. Linda was a year older than Patsi, who was twenty two, while Sharon was four years younger. We had had a few drinks then I invited them to my apt. for some weed. We all got high and laughed our heads off. I asked Patsi out later that week.

A few days after our date, I was sitting with Patsi and Sharon in the pub. I mentioned I had tickets for a local dance that Saturday and did she want to go. She said she was busy so I asked Sharon who said sure she would go. Patsi had been dating another guy for a while and they had plans for that weekend. She liked me so she had a dilemma of letting me take Sharon out and risk losing me or cancelling her date with the other guy. She chose to go to the dance with me.

Carol had dumped me by then so we started spending all our time together. Patsi had an apt. above the Irly Bird store where we partied all the time. After a month or so, I would occasionally stay over. Her father, Art, said that he didn't like seeing my motorcycle parked out front when he drove by in the morning. We either stayed at my place or I parked out of sight from then on.

About a month later we decided to take a motorcycle ride along the Washington coast, through central Oregon and ending in Reno. We spent the first night at a campground in Oregon. The next morning was nice and cool as we headed east towards Nevada. The closer to Reno we got, the temperature increased. By midday it was near 100 degrees and by two pm, near Susanville it was over 110. It was unbearable with the only relief from the wind in our faces. We came to spot where there was roadwork. A paving crew was working for about twenty miles, so we could only crawl along. The heat from the tar, added to the 110 degrees temp plus the heat from the bike made it feel like we were in an oven. Patsi had taken off her long sleeve shirt and rode with bare arms and shoulders. We arrived in Reno after another three hours, checked in to a hotel, and found that Patsi had a sever sunburn with large blisters all over her arms and shoulders. I found a pharmacy to get some relief for her. It was terrible night as she dealt with the pain. She was kind of loopy the next day but wanted to check out some casinos with me. There were free drinks at a bar so while I was playing roulette, she sat at the bar. The bartender gave her two Singapore Slings. It was too late when she found out that he had made them doubles. The drinks added to the sunstroke made for a pretty funny scene when she came over to the roulette table, demanding the pink chips, not settling for any other color, and lost them all in short order. I filled her with hot soup and coffee for the next few hours until she recovered.

We stayed for a couple days and then moved on into Northern California, heading towards Sacramento to get on the I-5 for our trip north. The first night we stayed in a small town where there was a hotel with a bar. We had packed Patsi's guitar so we fit into a great party that was going on. We stayed up late making lots of new friends.

In the morning, as we were packing up to leave, a few of our new friends came to see us off. Patsi got on the bike first. I got on and lifted the kickstand only to have my foot set down on some gravel. It slipped out to the side with the bike going down under me. Patsi fell, with her left foot getting caught under the bike. I was embarrassed as she yelled at me to get the bike off of her. While all these people watched, I picked the bike up, got her free, and back on the bike. I loaded Patsi, then myself and left town with my head hung low and with my pride in tatters.

When I got back from the motorcycle trip, I went to pick up my ICP check only to find the mailbox empty. I called the office and heard the GM tell me that I only got paid when I was in the territory. This was total bull, just a play on his part, as the schools were closed for the summer. On top of that it was not a salary but a draw against our commissions. I had worked with this company for six years and this was a first. I decided then that I wasn't going to work for anyone who had that kind of control over me again. I had some money and the fish and chip truck. I told them where to put their job and quit.

I had started to go to garage sales buying tools and then taking them to the flea market on Sunday mornings. I loved the second hand/auction business but I didn't have enough money to fill a store so I got the idea for a consignment store. I found a large location in an old beat up building on the main street of White Rock. The rent was $500 per month. We fixed it up as best as we could, got a large sign made and gave ourselves the name "CANADAWEST CONSIGNMENT SALES".

I wrote an ad in an editorial format, telling the story of how great a consignment store could be, explaining its advantage as a way to sell items for a maximum return. We would do all the work, saving the seller a lot of time by not having to be home to answer calls or to show the items. We charged a commission of 25%.

When it came to opening day, we had an empty store. We were hoping people would trust us with their goods. We saw a couple of people outside as we arrived to open the doors. It soon turned into a deluge with goods pouring in the doors. Trucks pulled up with dining room suites, sofa sets, appliances, musical instruments. Everything you used in a home was soon filling the store. It was unbelievable. We were placing the stuff as best as possible. Some of the people wanted so little for their goods that I would buy them for cash. We made some sales that day, but in a few days the store was almost filled.

It was a success from day one. I was having a ball. Patsi quit her job at Irly Bird to run the store so I could go out to pick up stuff (we charged a pickup fee) or go to auctions in Vancouver to buy goods in quantity. I loved the auctions as it brought back the memories of the pony auctions from my childhood.

I met a guy at the local auction who became a mentor to me. Don McDonald had been in the second hand business all his life, having taken over his father's Vancouver store on Main Street back in the fifties. He had sold out by the time I met him, but he was still buying to fill his son's store in Kamloops. Don was in his late forties, lived in a nice home with his wife Shirley and daughter Kelly. Don and I had a lot in common and he became like a father to me. Not only did we like to buy/sell, but we both drank scotch, a lot of scotch. We would sit in the back of the auctions sucking down a twenty sixer. After the auction we often went back to his place to drink some more and gamble, another similar vice we shared. Shirley put up with us as she had with Don all their married life. She was a saint.

The big test came one time when we both were hammered at the auction and a huge moose head came up for bid. We determined it would look "so good" in Don's basement so we bought it. I will always remember Shirley's face when she saw these two drunks at the door with a massive moose head. She said there was no way that THING was going in her home and it didn't. The darn thing became a mascot in my store. Shirley died a few years later leaving Don a very lonely guy for many years to come. I see my friend about once a year for a beer.

After a month or so the GM from ICP called and said he was coming to see me. He and the sales manager showed up at the store. I was glad I was busy at the time they arrived. They could see that I had a going concern for a business and wasn't going back to work for them. I said for them to come back to my place that night to pick up my samples, etc. When they walked away that night it ended a seven year odyssey working for a large corporation.

My anger was less visible, but it rose to the surface whenever I was near Marlene. We were at each other's throats every time we even talked on the phone. I would have to see her often as the fish truck was stored in the back of her house and in her basement was a freezer full of fish and chips. When we split, she got the house and it had really increased in value. I got a piece of property we owned in Ft. Frances. My mood was in the dump whenever she would come downstairs to complain about how much of an ass I was. Scott was acting up a lot and was having a real tough time in grade school. She wanted me to discipline him and I went overboard with spanking him. I was becoming like my father, exactly what I hated.

Patsi and I were living together in my apt. Pot was a very big part of our life with both of us smoking up as soon as we got home from work. Pot gives me the biggest case of the munchies the world has ever seen. We would do a joint followed by my need for snacks, which I never was smart enough to have on hand. I would call the local taxi to go to a small store, a mere block from home. He would come back with chips, cheezies, pop, ice cream, and more. The fish and chip truck was still working weekends and the store was making money so I wasn't thinking about cost.

On one occasion I pulled a two liter bottle of pop out of the door of the fridge, set it down on the counter, only to have it fall over on its side. I picked it up only to have it fall twice more. It was crazy watching this bottle that could not stand up. I called Patsi to come see. Set it up and over it would go. We both were laughing our heads off until I realized that when I pulled it from the fridge, the bottom of the bottle stayed behind. It would have taken a miracle for the bottle to stand on its round bottom.

A week or so later on a Sept. evening a friend and his lady came by with a bag of cocaine so we tried it for the first time. I liked it and so did Patsi. I thought I had just found a new way to party as it just made me feel so good. We were looking forward getting a supply for ourselves as soon as we could.

On the following Sat. we went to the bar as usual, got tipsy, and came home to bed. My life was about to change in the biggest possible way, but I was totally in the dark at that time. I was to undergo a metamorphosis. The old Ken was about to confront the truth of life. Nothing would ever be the same again.

THE END OF BOOK ONE

Book Two

Chapter Five

God Called Me By Name (Isaiah 41 Vs 1)

I had a slight leading of God in Winnipeg, but it soon dissipated. I was my own God and I never bowed down to anyone on earth. I had even told the priest when Scott was dedicated that I was not a believer and would not teach my son any of that garbage. He dedicated him anyway, more proof of my unbelief.

In the army we were made to attend church parade on Sunday mornings and I had been sent to Sunday school as a kid while my parents stayed home.

I had gone to church once with my mother when I was about 13 and even at that age I rebelled and told her I was not going back to hear some guy tell me how to live my life from reading from some book that was 1000's of years old.

I awoke around nine on a September Sunday morning feeling a little hung over, as always, and was going to have a shower and start the day. I swung my feet out of bed and the moment they touched the floor my life was changed.

A voice spoke to me as audible as if a radio or a TV had been turned on. It said,

"KEN - THAT IS A FAR AS I AM GOING TO LET YOU GO. EITHER YOU SERVE ME OR SERVE THE WORLD. TODAY YOU CHOOSE!"

I was transformed in a second from a non-believer to a believer. I knew what I had heard and I knew who had said it. He called me by my name. He knew me all along, all my life He had been there.

Why me, why then? I didn't know and I didn't even want to think about it. When God touches you, all rational thinking is gone. All I knew is that I had to find Him that day, that Sunday morning; I had to get to a church now. I didn't tell Patsi anything; I just got up, showered, dressed and hit the door to find God.

There are a lot of churches in White Rock, BC and I didn't have a clue what the difference was between them. There was Protestant, Catholic, Jehovah Witness, Mormon, Christian Science and more. I would have gone to any one that was open at that time, about 9:30am.

I started my journey with the closest church only to find it didn't have a service until 11:00 am. So I continued on around town only to find that each building was closed. I went to the next community, same thing, and then to another. All were starting later and I didn't know what to do so I headed for home as it was a little after 10am. On the last road into White Rock, on the left hand side, there was a small building with cars in the parking lot and others pulling in. There was a name above the door -WHITE ROCK TABERNACLE. I knew that was a faith name of some kind, and had to decide if I was going in or not. It was a hard decision as I sat in the parking lot. I was worried about going into a strange place where I knew no one, but He drew me and in I went.

The service was in full swing as I slipped into the last pew by myself. No one looked at me and after I couple minutes, the fear went away. I stood up when asked to and listened to the music. I started to observe the other people and saw a look upon their faces like I had never seen before. There was a sense of joy coming from all around the building, as they seemed drawn into a new world or presence. Many had their arms raised and some were even dancing in the aisles. It was both terrifying and exhilarating at the same time, I knew I was in the presence of God and that these people had something that I needed and wanted. I stayed until about 11:45, leaving before the service was over, to go open my store.

I didn't think anyone had seen me there and I can't remember much about the rest of the day but things started to happen after I had told Patsi. The next day in the store the pastor, Vern Wilson, came to say hello and offered to take me for a coffee. That began a friendship that lasted almost fifteen years until he died. He just wanted to get to know me and didn't preach at me ever. My vocabulary contained a lot of words that would offend any sane person, but not Vern. He just smiled when one would slip out and carry on as if it hadn't happened. Such wisdom on his part and I eventually was able to push the delete button on the f word and add a few new forms of exclamations.

Patsi was working with me in the store and didn't like what was happening as one after another Christian would come by the store to encourage me, saying hello to her. She would soon recognize them as they returned and would quickly pick up the telephone; as if she was busy to avoid having to talk to them. Many came by, but two in particular joined Vern in having a huge effect on me. One was Jacob Schurman who was a local hairdresser. Jacob was as opposite of me as you can get. I was loud and boisterous while he was quite and calm. I was big and he was small. He was a hairdresser and I WASN"T. A hairdresser - you have got to be kidding me. I was a tough guy who rode motorcycles, fought in bars, smoked pot and drank like a fish while this little man worked at the Pink Palace (no joke) the Pink "freakin" Palace and he kept asking me to go to lunch with him. It kind of became a joke with Patsi and me. God sure must have a sense of humor to set this up. There was not a chance that I was going for lunch with him, but he persisted and finally one day he said there was a banquet in Surrey on Friday evening that he and his wife were going to. He had an extra ticket that I could have. In my world a banquet meant a lot to eat and I always was up for good food in quantity.

When Friday evening came they came and picked me up. There must have been a lot of hungry people in Surrey that Friday night as the room was full of tables with eight people sitting with knives and forks at the ready position, at each table.

Someone welcomed us all, said grace, and the feast began. I really don't remember much about the meal or the people at our table. I remember nothing until a speaker was introduced. I listened carelessly at first and then paid more attention as he shared his life story - HE LIVED THE SAME LIFE AS ME - EXACTLY - BOOZE - WOMEN – DIVORCE - DRUGS. He knew me in every way, all my dirty secrets, my failures, my guilt, and shame. The pain I had caused others. He told his story and shared his regrets.

He then explained how he came to realize that Jesus loved him even while he had been doing all those things that caused so much pain to those in his life. That sin separates all men from God's presence. Then he said that all of his sins had been forgiven by God, because God had made a way for all mankind to be saved. God had His Son, Jesus, pay the price for our sins. Jesus had come to earth as a man and lived a life without sin. And because He was without sin, we all could come to God and have a personal relationship with Him, if we would confess our sins and just believe in Him as God.

In other words, there had to be a price for our sins, but Jesus, God's Son paid the price on a cross, dying in our place so that we could come to know God and live with Him forever.

He continued by saying this gift of God was available to all believers and that a person could become right with God that very night. He asked if anyone in the room would like to ask God to come into their life, have their sins forgiven, and start a new life as a Christian, a follower of Christ.

We had all been asked to close our eyes before he asked for anyone who wanted to receive this gift to raise their hand. I was confident that no one would see me if I did, so I quickly shot min up high. A second later I knew I had been seen as all around the table I heard people saying "Praise the Lord" and "Thank you, Jesus."

The speaker then asked for those who had raised their hands to stand. I, with fear and trepidation, stood fully expecting tons of people to rise, but – OH, NO! – JUST ME!

He then asked me to come forward and I had no choice but to do so. The fear was leaving as I started to realize this was all part of God's plan.

The speaker laid his hands on my shoulder and asked me to repeat a prayer

I prayed, "Jesus, I am a sinner.

I ask you to please forgive me of my sins.

Would you please come into my life?

I want to serve you forever.

I believe you are God and you died for my sins.

Thank you."

I prayed and He came in!!!

I realized that God loved me so much that He orchestrated the last few weeks to bring me to this place on this evening to hear this speaker. God gave me a personal banquet that night as I was the only person who raised their hand that night.

I am forever grateful. I know I just took to preaching there, but there is no other way to explain what happened to me that night. "I once was lost, but now I'm found."

I wish I could tell you I lost all my bad habits that day. No, that didn't happen, but things started to change. The first to go was the weed. It took a few months but the desire to get high slowly evaporated. The problem was that it didn't for Patsi causing a rift between us. It didn't last long and we were both soon smoke free.

I started to attend the church every Sunday morning leaving Patsi at home to sleep in. She didn't show any interest in my Christianity, especially when I became a fanatic. I had such a life changing experience I couldn't stop talking about it. I was driving everyone around me nuts. My parents were concerned as they thought I had joined a cult. They called Vern to find out what had happened to me. He calmed them down and just kept taking me for coffee.

The men of the church met for prayer every Friday morning at six am. What an experience that was. I always thought prayer was a quiet time with your head bowed but – OH, NO! NO! NO! NOT IN THIS

CHURCH. God had brought me to a charismatic non-denominational body. They believed in the gifts of the spirit, praying out loud, and sometimes in the spirit with a new language. My head was in a daze, but my spirit was on fire. I was experiencing the presence of God in my life and I wanted it all.

More and more people would come by the store to encourage me. The one who was to become an important part of my story was Fred Vance. He had come to the Lord a few years earlier in a similar way as I did. He would take me to meetings and different church services. I saw that a lot of people were Christians from many different denominations, worshipping God in many unique ways.

While attending one service with Fred, I was really into the worship as were most of the others. Many had their hands raised and I wanted to raise mine but didn't have the nerve. As I struggled over this, I actually felt a hand push my arm into the air. I looked to see who did it. THERE WAS NO ONE THERE! All I know was that my hand was in the air and I didn't have any fear about that ever again.

Fred got to know Patsi, who was starting to show some interest in what was happening to me. Fred started to share with her and her sister Linda. They both asked Jesus into their lives during the next few weeks. They didn't get as crazy as me, but the seed was planted.

This all happened in the fall of 1979. The business was growing every day. I was now getting calls to see estates every week. We would explain how our system worked by selling on consignment. We would often be asked to make a cash offer which would often be accepted. Our inventory was growing every week, which transferred into more sales.

I was working hard one day when my foot started to hurt. The next day the pain was in my toe and felt like a ton of bricks fell on it. I could hardly walk so I was sitting on a sofa with my foot on a stool when a lady went by and hit my foot. I forgot I was a Christian as I screamed out in pain and used some words that would have made your ears curl. That poor lady was so sorry. That was my first experience with gout. It wasn't my last.

Patsi and I were doing well, but some of the ladies in the church thought I should reconcile with Marlene. They called her and she shut them down in a hurry. Their action did not endear them to Patsi, but later she understood why they did it.

Our life was continuing on, minus the dope. We were still having a few drinks. We were still working our heads off.

The local auction was owned by two ex CFL players, Keith Bennett and Billy Horty. These two were hard drinking, hard partying dudes. They were having a tough time working together so Keith left. He came by to see if I could use some help. I made another of my hundreds of mistakes by saying yes. Keith was a very opinionated guy so it wasn't long until we started to butt heads. We were much the same, with similar personalities. We both were hotheads who could blow at any time without too much provocation. I guess I learned what happened at the auction. The bottom line was that it was my business. I let him go after about three weeks of hell.

During the time Keith was there, a long time football friend of his started to hang around. He had been a lineman for the Blue Bombers in the late 50's and came to White Rock to buy real estate. I forget his last name, but his first name was Morley. Morley was big. He was real big. He was 6'5" or so weighing around 350. He also was mean.

I had bought an estate that had a pair of high-end binoculars in it. I had put them behind the counter as I intended to keep them for myself, but he was insisting I sell them to him. He was getting angrier every time he was in the store. He finally threatened me, so I had to either sell them to him or convince him to leave me alone. I had a realistic looking pellet gun pistol at the apt., so what I did was to call and asked him to come and meet me at the store. I had put the gun in a paper lunch bag and set it on a sofa table with just a bit of the grip showing out of the bag. I was sitting in the sofa with the bag just over my right shoulder. Morley came storming into the store, came over to where I was, and sat down in the chair across from where I was sitting. I told him he had to lay off or I was going to have to do something about it. He laughed and smirked, telling me I was gutless. He then spotted the pistol. I think he peed his pants. He started to shake and stutter. He left the store and never came back.

Patsi and I got the kids for a few weekends when Marlene wanted some time off. We did our best, but the kids didn't bond with Patsi and never would.

I was growing in my faith walk. I had a long way to go, but I was now a believer. God would reveal himself to me in some unusual ways. One day while I was driving back from Vancouver I was daydreaming. My friend Kalanchuck had become a radio announcer in Calgary. I was thinking what it would be like to be interviewed by him. In my mind, Bill asked, "So Ken, what's new in your life?" I would reply, "Well Bill, I have become a Christian." His response was, "What exactly does that mean?" and I was dumbfounded. I didn't have an answer. I then heard a voice inside say "Turn on your radio." It was tuned to a faith station and out of the speaker came these words, "A Christian is someone who has surrendered his life to Christ. They have acknowledged they are a sinner, in need of a saviour. They have confessed their sins and asked Jesus to forgive them." I was surprised, but I was starting to have this kind of relationship with God.

After about a year in business, a couple started to hang around the store and were asking a lot of questions. In a couple of months they started to talk about buying the business. They finally offered $25,000 plus the value of the inventory. It added up to $50,000.00. I never had that much in cash in my life. This was in 1980. The energy crisis was in full steam with a lot of articles in the paper about how wood burning stoves were the solution for heating homes, especially in the provinces that had severe, cold winters. The couple made an offer of $25,000 cash and a hundred acre woodlot in Bobcagen, Ont., about forty miles from Peterborough. My father had a wood stove business so I asked his opinion. He said that everyone in his area was burning wood and that it was a no brainer. I asked him to check out the lot and he came back with a positive report.

We sold the business with the closing falling on the thirtieth of November 1980. It would prove to be a huge mistake. If I had only realized that we had made our living for the year, paid all expenses, and had increased the inventory from zero to $25,000 in a year, I would never had sold but I was blinded by the $50,000 number.

I was intrigued by the auction business and decided that I wanted to become an auctioneer. I bought a course by mail that included a tape, teaching you the very basics to creating a proper auction chant. I spent hours and hours going...1 1 bid 2- 2 2 bid 3- 3 3 bid 4. It taught how to get your numbers in order so you could run from 1 to 10 then 10 to 1 over and over. I worked on it for weeks driving Patsi crazy. After you get the bid down you start to add fillers...1 bid 2 go 2 now 2 hear 2 say 2 then 2 go 3 now 3 hear 3 say, go, bid, hear, come along, let's go to... It all started to roll off my tongue. I would practice every day for hours until I sounded like some of those guys who sold the ponies when I was a kid.

As soon as I had the cash in hand, I went and bought a brand new Dodge PU truck. It was a short box with the wide fenders. Real sweet. We then decided to go to Ontario to see my family and to buy a cargo truck, fill it with a load of antiques and haul it all back to BC, to sell them at Semiahmoo Antique Auctions. I made arrangements with the auction owner, Wally Dodds before we flew to Ontario. We got to Peterborough to stay at my parents. They had met Patsi when they had come out in the previous summer. I bought a five ton truck and started going to all the local auctions in the Peterborough area to fill it up. It took about three weeks.

My sister Anne was living in a town close by and Carol was in Peterborough when my brother Hal showed up out of nowhere. Hal was a complete mess. He was hooked on hard drugs, including acid, and his brain was fried. He was so out of it.

He was telling us all about secret army bases all over Canada that were setting up to attack all the civilians. Everything he said or thought was insane. He was so paranoid that he thought everyone was out to kill him. It was driving my parents nuts. My father made a string alarm on the stairs in case Hal tried to come up at night to kill all of us. We were living in a madhouse.

We wanted to get away from the craziness asap. We also needed to get back to BC for the auction to sell the load. I had installed an extra gas tank on the truck so we would be sure to never run out of gas on a stretch of prairie hwy. The trip started out uneventful but long. After four days we were crossing Saskatchewan on the Trans Canada Hwy. The temp outside was around minus twenty five with wind blowing the snow so hard it was difficult to see. It seemed like we were the only vehicle on the hwy as we had not seen anyone for a long time.

The truck had run well but all of a sudden I noticed a miss. In less than a minute the truck started to sputter and then it stopped altogether. I went out in the cold, freezing wind to look in the gas tank. It was possible to see in them as they were attached to the side of the truck. One was bone dry while the other had gas in it. The original tank was a twenty gallon. The one I added held thirty gallons. The guy who installed it had run a rubber tube from one tank to the other to balance the usage. It was a mistake because when the twenty gallon tank was empty (meaning we had used twenty gallons from each tank) the tube created a vacuum and was only sucking air. The gas could not flow from the thirty gallon tank into the carburetor. I learned all this while looking at the system. Patsi was in the truck without heat and was starting to freeze. I was already freezing outside. I realized first that we were in big trouble and second there was no one to help. I must have prayed because the solution came to me. I needed to disconnect the twenty gallon tank from the thirty. Easy enough to do by just disconnecting the hose from the twenty, which I did. I then realized that I now had a hose with no way to plug it. After a minute I remembered the bubblegum we had bought. Patsi started to chew like crazy. In a minute or so it was pliable, so I covered up the end of the tube with it. It froze in about ten seconds and made a solid bond. I then siphoned a pop can full of gas from the tank and poured it into the carburetor, hit the starter, and in a minute it roared to life.

We made it to the next town without seeing anyone on the road, filled up both tanks, reconnected the tube and now realized that I only had forty gallons available. If you ever need any help with a fuel problem just call me.

We made it back to White Rock and unloaded the antiques at the auction. We sold the truck for what I had paid for it. The day of the auction arrived only to see us break even on the sale of the goods. A lot of work not to make any money, but we learned a lot of lessons.

My parents were out of their mind with Hal so they gave him some money and a bus ticket back to BC. He was supposed to call me when he arrived, but I never got a call. If he made it to BC, I never heard. No one has ever heard from him again. There has never been a sighting, nothing. My parents made every kind of inquiry possible and made missing person reports everywhere and to every police dept. they could. They contacted the Salvation Army who has a missing person bureau. My mother was desperate with worry. They came to BC a couple of times over the next few years searching around a couple of Indian reserves they knew he had spent time at, without any success. Hal had disappeared off the face of the earth. My parents came to accept his disappearance, but really wanted to have closure. They never were to get what they wanted.

Chapter Six

I'm An Auctioneer – 25 Bid 30 Dollars Sir

I had a friend who had an auction in Surrey. He convinced me that the Fraser Valley needed another auction and Abbotsford was the place to go. We found a new building with about 3000 sq. ft. next to Buns Master. The landlords were great guys who took a liking to us. They gave us a great deal and we were off. It took around two months to make the location into an auction. The biggest job was building the stage and the bleachers. We set it up to hold about 200 people. We worked hard, doing all of the physical labor ourselves. We also had to get the inventory to set up for the first auction.

There was no way to have your first auction without having it filled with exciting goods so I would go to auctions in Vancouver two days a week, buying as much as possible. I was also buying in Abbotsford from calls we were getting from our ads.

I soon realized I had made a big mistake buying the pickup truck. I had side racks made for it with large signs on both sides, but I would still have to make two or three trips to get all that I had bought. I decided we needed a cargo van so I started to call all the car dealership in town. Was I ever in for a shock.

This was early in1981 and Chrysler had just gone broke. No one, and I mean no one, was buying a Chrysler product. I went from thinking it would a piece of cake to find a used van where I could trade the in the PU, to being desperate as the days dragged on. Now I was doing the auction build, buying stock, and trying to buy a van. I was tired, angry, and getting depressed. It got so bad that I was down to almost giving the PU away to get a van.

I found a guy with an older post office truck who would trade with me and give me $2000. That would mean about a $5000 dollar loss. There was no other option, so I was on my way to see the van when I heard THE VOICE say, "DO NOT GO THERE." I said, "Okay, I will just look at it and leave." HE SAID, "DO NOT GO THERE!" I said, "Ok, I will just tell him I'm not interested." The third time He spoke I finally got the message. I turned right at the next road and drove away from there as fast I could go. I am sorry Lord for being so stupid, and I thank you for not giving up on me.

Later that night Patsi and I were having supper in a restaurant in Abbotsford. We were going to an auction in Mission so we decided to stay in Abbotsford and not go back to Surrey. As we ate I noticed the Ford dealer across from the restaurant that I had not visited in my search. We ate and went to the lot. I heard the same story as everywhere else, but he said there was another Ford dealer in Chilliwack that had a cube van and might make a deal. It was only five pm, so with the auction still two hours away, we set out for Chilliwack. He had given me the directions to Chilliwack Ford, which was on the main drive. We pulled off the freeway, turning onto the main drag. We were making our way along the street looking for the Ford sign, when I saw a Chrysler lot on my left. I decided to check it out before going to the Ford dealership. As we entered I saw a cube van on my right next to the parking stalls. I had not even turned off the engine when the doors of the showroom burst open and a guy comes running out to my window. He yells, "I hope you want to sell this truck because I have a buyer for it!" I got my senses back in a moment and casually replied, "I might."

The story gets really weird now when I asked about the cube van. It was brand new and had been ordered for the local Hostess potato chip salesman. On Saturday the chip guy came to pick it up. He jumped into the back walked around and as he turned to go out the back, he hit his head on the roll up door. He hit it hard as he was six feet tall. He stormed out of the truck, telling them to stick it. I am five feet ten and walked under the door without a problem. The end of this is crazy but that is how God works sometimes. They brought out the invoice showing it cost the dealer $14,000 for the van. They were having a tough time as were all Chrysler dealers. They sold me the van for the $14,000 and gave me...wait for it... ALL MY MONEY BACK FOR THE PICK UP. This is not a misprint. This is how God can bless. He even did it even when I was so stupid as to take three times to obey. I signed the papers, came back the next day with a certified check and a faith that just kept growing. THANK YOU JESUS.

I took the truck to a sign painter friend and had in emblazoned with "PACIFIC COAST AUCTIONS". As well as the address and telephone number, it had four small phrases on the bottom panel, two were normal and two said, "Praise the Lord"

We were in the Bible belt so no one ever questioned my expressions.

When it came auction day for our first sale, I was feeling really sick. We had over 10,000 dollars sitting on the stage with no guarantee we would get it back as there is nothing that can kill an auction faster than putting reserves on items. I determined to sell everything on the stage for the top bid. Everything was going to be sold. I also knew that a person who gets a good deal always comes back and he tells all of his friends.

Just before the sale began I was outside the back door throwing up. My nerves were stretched and stretching more as the clock moved toward seven pm. We thanked everyone for coming and started. I sold my first item, breaking the ice, and we were in the auction business. At the end of the night we had made some money, selling everything we had. The auction world is tough because it is so labor intensive. The auction itself is a lot of fun for three or four hours, but then we are back to work hauling the furniture out to the waiting cars and trucks. We would finish around eleven or twelve pm, go out for something to eat, and get to bed after the adrenaline would dissipate.

After a year in Abbottsford Patsi and I decided to buy a small mobile home in a trailer park. It was old, but a cheap way to live. We had been together for almost two years without ever mentioning marriage. In the middle of the night God woke me up, telling me to get out of bed. He told me I was not to sleep with Patsi anymore. I obeyed and moved into the second bedroom. In the morning Patsi asked why I had done that. I told her what God had told me. She was anything but impressed by how holy I thought I was. In two days she had packed up and moved home. I had told her we had to get married if we wanted to stay together. It took her about a week to get her head around that idea. She moved back and we stayed apart We talked to the pastors at the Rhema Faith Centre who told us we had to take marriage counseling before they would marry us. The permanent pastors were in there early fifties but had gone on a sabbatical for a few months. They had left Ken and Shar Gretter, both in their early twenties, in charge. They were very nice, strong believers who had attended bible school, but they were so innocent. They had no idea of where I had come from, but we worked through the course with them. We were married on the twenty forth of January, 2003. It was just a service with two people as witnesses. Patsi hadn't told anyone in her family so I guess you could say we eloped. She kept it a secret for almost three months until her conscience couldn't take it anymore. They were less than excited, but accepted the fact that it was done.

After a few months we decided to open a consignment store to compliment the auction. There was an open space at the other end of our bldg. We needed someone to run it so we called Fred Vance. When I had first meet Fred he was selling furniture for K&D Furniture in White Rock. We offered a salary with commission so he said he would help us out. We also stocked the consignment store with goods we had bought. A funny thing happened for Fred's first sale. We had some porcelain items and a lady came in to browse through the store. She picked up a small duck and brought it up to Fred to pay for it. We thought it would be good to get buyers names and so he asked her name. When the lady replied, "MRS. QUACK", Fred had to pick himself off the floor from laughing so hard.

Patsi's walk with God had not grown too much during this time. I was attending church each Sunday and she would come with me sometimes but was very intimidated by the move of the Spirit. When Fred arrived we started to have Bible studies with the three of us in the consignment store after work. We would sit in comfortable chairs and he would read scripture and then give a context to it.

On one stormy evening he told us a story about an evangelist in Africa. He had been holding a meeting in a meadow next to an African village. The whole village gathered to hear him. There was so much interest in his message that the local witch doctor became intimidated. He decided to have his cronies disrupt the meeting by encircling the area, beat on drums to chase a pride of lions into the meadow. The lions entered causing uproar among the people. The evangelist asked God to send lightening to stop the lions and the Lord answered with a bolt of lightning killing a lion. WHAT HAPPENED NEXT CHANGE PATSI'S LIFE...BECAUSE AT THE EXACT MOMENT FRED SAID "THE LORD SENT A LIGHTNING BOLT", LIGHTNING RATTLED THE BACK DOOR OF OUR BLDG...TRUTH...IT HAPPENED JUST AS I HAVE WRITTEN IT. Fred lifted his head, smiled for a second, picked up his book and carried on. Patsi and my eyes were as big as saucers. Patsi made another decision for the Lord that night with a whole lot of conviction that has lasted all these years.

The auction was doing well, but it sure took a lot more work than we ever planned on. I needed some time off. I always liked to fish so I convinced Patsi that if we had a camper to fit on my pickup truck, we could travel. I especially wanted to go up the Sunshine Coast to Pender Harbor, which was a world class salmon fishing location. We bought the camper and we were off. A girl who worked for us came alone to keep Patsi company, while I fished for dinner. I rented a twelve ft. aluminum with a twenty five hp outboard for four days. I had the equipment but knew none of the methods necessary for catching the big ones.

I headed out on day one, fishing in a small bay just outside the harbor with several other boats. I had live bait in a large pail that I had to keep adding fresh water to so they would stay alive. Many fish come into the other boats, but I was skunked and came in empty handed. Day two came and I was among the same crowd. I finally got some hits, bringing one to the edge of the boat only to have it slip off before I could land it. I was desperate as I was the only guy in the camp without a fish to BBQ. I was hopeless as a fisherman. It was getting time to go in when a guy who fished near me came over and gave me a fish. I couldn't believe it. I was so excited I headed back to camp to show the girls. I had to go by our campsite on the way to the dock. I held up the fish and hollered for them to light the BBQ. I docked the boat, put the rods on the dock, next the tackle box, and then the fish. As I reached for the lifejacket, the fish rolled off the dock, into the water and started to sink. I jumped in after it, following it as it sank to the bottom. I lost it. I lost the darn fish. I almost cried as I walked back up to the campsite to face my shame. We ate beans again that night as the girls stared longingly at the next site where BBQ salmon was on the menu. I caught two salmon myself the next day and all was forgiven.

I now felt I was qualified to fish so I started to look for a boat. I finally found one a little bigger than I should have. It was a twenty two ft. cuddy cabin with a small head and a stove. I was nuts thinking I could handle this and soon proved it. It came with a trailer so I hooked it up, loaded Scott and a guy named Dean, who worked for me, on a Friday at six pm and headed for Pender Harbor via the ferry terminal to the Sunshine Coast. Our plan was to get to the camp by midnight, sleep in the boat and get up to launch at daybreak. We awoke in the cool dew of morning. I had parked by the boat launch so we were ready to go. I unhooked the tie downs and backed the trailer until the boat was in the water. I put the emergency brake on, jumped out, and headed down the length of the trailer to climb into the boat. Dean loosened the hook from the tow wire to let the boat float out, before he jumped into car to park it. They went over to the dock where I would pick them up.

I got the boat running, put it into gear, and headed out. I went about ten ft. and ended up on top of a huge submerged rock. The boat was balanced on the middle of the rock with about six ins. of the boat in the water and the rest sitting high and dry. After I realized what had happened and let out a few choice words, I turned off the motor and slipped over the side onto the rock. I headed to the front while hanging on to the side of the boat. I inched around reaching the bow. With my feet on the rock, I got my shoulder under the boat and shoved as hard as I could. The boat moved off the rock a lot easier and faster than I thought it would. It slipped off and I made a grab for the rail, just catching it before it got away. I was dragging at about a forty five degree angle with my feet hanging out behind me as the boat became free and floating.

I moved around to the back where I could climb back aboard. Scott and Dean were going crazy laughing at me as I pulled the boat into the dock. I mean I hit the dock. I tried to put the gear into neutral but hit reverse instead taking about of six inches of plank off the dock. I now had to take the boat to the shop for a new prop. I was into the trip for a few hundred before a line was in the water. We started to fish later that morning and we landed two springs over twenty five lbs. each.

I was still attending the auctions in Vancouver, buying deals, and bringing them back to our sale. We had customers from all over, even some dealers from upcountry, so I would buy with them in mind. If they could fill their truck at my sale; they didn't have to go anywhere else. We had one competitor in town. We got along well and would help each other whenever it was needed. I even let the owner use my auction course to make him a better auctioneer. We worked so hard every week, starting over the next day after the sale. Week after week we had to find more stock. It was very physical labor and I would wear out every couple of months or so.

Abbotsford is the Bible Belt of Canada with thousands of Mennonites having settled in the area to farm the incredible dirt of the Fraser Valley. There are more churches per capita than anywhere else in BC. There was always a great reception to any move of God in the area so when an evangelist named Len Lindstrom set up a huge tent and held revival meeting for about two weeks, I had to attend. I went with Jonas Mellon, a friend from Full Gospel Businessmen International. We went and sat on a bench near the back of the sawdust covered ground. It was a wonderful gospel word with an alter call at the end. I didn't want to go forward, but Jonas did and he convinced me to go up with him. We all stood in a long line as the evangelist moved along the line praying for each person.

Some of the people were falling down, but that wasn't for me. As he came closer I prepared myself. Jonas hit the ground like a brick as soon as he touched him. That was enough for me, but he got to me before I could move. He did not touch me but put his hands about four inches away from my ears on both sides. He said, "IN JESUS NAME" and I was down. My legs became like mush. All I know was that it was the most wonderful feeling in the world. A peace came over me that I didn't want to end. It finally felt like it lifted and I got up.

I was surprised one day to learn another auction company was coming to town. The owners were an uncle and his nephew. I learned the uncle had had an auction in another province earlier so I did some investigation. I found out that he had been tossed out of the province after having done some indiscretions. When he heard I had checked him out, he called and told me he was going to kill me. I had to deal with this idiot for the next two years. We were at war. We would compete for every estate deal in town. He had leased two new Cadillac's, a new five ton truck, and a semi truck and trailer. He would buy container loads of furniture from American manufacturers, open them, smash some items, and then close the container again. He would then video himself opening the container and finding the damaged goods. He would then refuse to pay the seller, sell the load, and pocket the money. We were a small town auction up against a world class crook and we had a tough time competing against him. There was a second hand dealer in town that had a stroke. His wife asked them to sell the goods, which they did. The problem was they never paid the wife for the goods. He was buying huge deals, loading his semi, and heading all over the province holding sales. He rented a home in the most expensive gated community in town. The police knew what he was doing, but the uncle had a famous Vancouver lawyer on retainer to get him out of trouble. I was losing more ground to him every day. People who knew what was happening stayed with us, but we couldn't compete with the money he had to use. I finally lowered our commission from 25% to

10% to sell and introduced a 10% buyer's premium. Everyone said I was nuts, but all the major auctions in Vancouver had done it and I felt it was a way to set ourselves apart from him. We told the buyers for three sales what was to come so when the first sale with the buyer's premium happened, I was terrified. I thought they would show their displeasure by not bidding and that is exactly what they did. The first item that should have sold for thirteen to fifteen dollars brought five. The next was about the same and the third too. Then it broke as they could not help themselves watching the stuff sell for less then they knew it was worth. By the end of the sale all was forgiven. It actually worked for the buyer's advantage because we would get more items to sell by charging a smaller commission to the seller.

We did a lot of auctions over the years, but a few really stand out. One was the result of a horrible tragedy. A man killed his wife and then committed suicide. They were well known in town for running a high-end hair salon. There was huge media coverage so when the executor asked us to do the auction it became the biggest auction in our time in Abbotsford. We sold boats, snowmobiles, cars, everything they had. The auction room was so full that the fire marshal came and we had to shut down for a while to make some space. The sale grossed over $50,000 when our average sale did around $10,000. The sale ended late and the staff was all in the office. It was around one am when there was a pounding on the front door that was now locked. I went to see who it was. I didn't recognize him. He said he left something during the sale, wanting to pick it up. I thought he looked a little sketchy so I said for him to come back in the morning. I then called the police to escort me to the bank. We were playing it safe with so much money. A friend of mine was robbed a few years later when someone followed him from his sale to the bank.

Another time an older lady had passed away and the son called us to do the sale. I went to the home to make the arrangements. It was so weird because the son's sister was also there and they seemed to hate each other. They could not agree on anything. Every time the one wanted to keep an item for themselves the other would want it too. It got so ridiculous that they finally decided that everything would go to auction where they would just bid against each other. I was delighted. Neither of them took one thing. It was all for me to sell. Auction day arrived. It was a payday for sure. Whenever one of them would bid on an item, the other would drive the price to somewhere over retail. Over and over it went. The public was in awe as every item went for a crazy price. The strangest item was one of those mini trampolines called a rebounder. It was an exerciser that was sold by home sales. The daughter had sold one to the mother for $400 (we sold them for around twenty dollars anytime we got one). When it came up I started the bidding at ten dollars. Someone in the crowd held up their paddle and the daughter bid twenty. I thought it was done, but the other lady bid again and then so did the daughter. Again and again, back and forth the bidding went until it got over $300 and was knocked down to the daughter. She had arranged for a friend to come and bid against her, to save face, because her brother had accused her of cheating her mother for selling it to her.

We made page two of the Vancouver Sun with a sale we did for a lawyer friend from White Rock. He had a client who owned a lot of commercial property around town. One tenant had a pet store with a lot of fish, birds, mice, etc. He had walked out of the store owing rent so we were hired to sell what was left to recover some of the money. When we got to the store I found a cage open with a sign reading, "Python". I HATE SNAKES. I can handle a lot of situations, but I'm like a little girl when it comes to snakes. After a few minutes I knew how to get free advertising for the sale. I called the Vancouver Sun, telling them that I have to do this sale, but there is a snake loose in the store. They bit and sent a photographer out right away. Before they arrived, we found the snake curled up in a corner. The photographer wanted me to pick up the snake for a picture. What a dilemma, a picture in the Sun creating a big auction or zip. As I write this I can still look up and see a framed copy of that picture hanging on the wall. I had lots of dark curly hair and a beard back then. This three foot snake is moving up and down and I grabbed it about the halfway mark. The picture shows the snake trying to get at my nose. The sale was a success.

Shortly after one of the guys we had rented the building from built a new home just north of town and offered it to us for $80,000. We came up with the $10,000 down and got a mortgage from the local credit union. It was a beautiful three bedroom with a full basement. Patsi loved it.

Marlene and I had come to an understanding that we would get the kids every second weekend. It gave me a chance to be a father but it was so difficult because they were never able to bond with Patsi. I guess they blamed her for the family breakup but she was innocent of that. I met her after the marriage had ended but before the divorce papers were filed. She tried to deal with it, but it would blow up every so often. It often ended with some kind of disagreement, with the kids being defiant, rejecting her position and I would be in trouble with their mother when I took them home. On one occasion it was only Cindy who came. On the Sunday evening I drove her home in the cube van. When we got to her house, I kissed her goodbye and left. As I drove along the hwy towards home, I heard a loud banshee screen and something jumped on my neck. I froze in fear as claws dug into my skin. I reached behind my head, grabbing the fur of Cindy's cat. My heart raced for a moment until I could grasp what was happening. That dumb cat must have jumped into the truck when I had dropped Cindy as her house. The kids thought it was hilarious, I didn't.

During my annual physical the doctor discovered a small problem, saying I would need a small surgery to prevent it from becoming more serious. The day came for the operation. A friend came and prayed with me just before I was given the shot to make you relax as you go into the operating room. I was soon put under the anesthesia. During the time I was under the most terrifying thing ever happened to me. I sensed I was falling into a pit of darkness where an evil voice started to curse me with the foulest curses you can imagine. He told me, "NOW I GOT YOU, YOU SOB - I HATE YOU!" He used every foul word possible over and over again. I kept falling deeper and deeper into the abyss that was bottomless. There was no let up as it seemed to go on forever. Finally, as I started to come out of the anesthesia in the recovery room, I was yelling at the nurse, "DID I DIE?" I wanted to know if I had died and was resuscitated during the operation. Had I actually gone to hell?

I had had an encounter with Satan. I instantly went into a deep depression because I didn't know why God allowed this to happen. I was really angry at God. I was a Christian so how did the devil have the right to do that to me. This threw me for a loop and my faith was put to the test. I knew what had happened was not a dream but a reality. I needed an answer there wasn't one.

About two weeks later I was sound asleep in the middle of the night. I experienced the whole thing again. It all came back. I was falling into the pit as before with the cursing demon tormenting me as I went down further and further. Fear raged, as I was screaming in my sleep, trying to wake up. When I finally woke, the whole thing continued. I was now awake and still falling with curses raining down on me. It was not a dream but was really happening. I was overwhelmed and started screaming out loud for God to help me. I ran for my Bible on the coffee table in the living room. I was crying for God's help. I flung opened the bible and read the first verse I could see. It said, "DEMONS MUST FLEE AT THE NAME OF JESUS". I started to proclaim HIS name over and over. God had given me the weapon to fight the enemy with. I declared it louder and louder, over and over. "JESUS !!! JESUS !!! JESUS !!! BEGONE IN THE NAME OF JESUS. The enemy lifted off me after the longest two or three minutes of my life. My nerves were shot. I was shaking as I wiped the tears from my eyes. I had just experienced the power and authority of the name of JESUS.

Somehow I went back to bed, eventually falling asleep. The attack came back as strong as before, but this time I woke up quickly and made the proclamation "BEGONE IN THE NAME OF JESUS". This attack lasted only about sixty seconds until it ended. It came again two more times that night, ending sooner each time. My faith was being built into a strong tower all night long. In the morning, as I awoke, I sensed the presence of a demon sitting on the windowsill. It came off the sill and landed on my chest. I started to laugh. After what had happened all night I knew that the demon was defeated and had to go. I just said, "Be gone in Jesus name." and it left, never to come again. God had allowed the whole experience to teach me the power of His Name. I have walked in that knowledge since that day. When He died on the cross, Satan was defeated. We have been set free. His ties have been broken. We can walk in God's authority and by the power of His Name thru any adversity we may face. All creation is subject to the power of His name. "JESUS" "JESUS" "JESUS" every knee shall bow and tongue confess that Jesus is Lord. Amen.

It is difficult to write about worldly life and spiritual life together, bouncing back and forth between the two, but that is what I need to do.

In 1983, CKVU, a local television station in Vancouver, wanted to do a television show on auctioneers. They chose Ken from Fraser Valley Livestock Auctions, Loves Auctions, a century old company in downtown Vancouver, and they choose us. Wow. They featured each auction for a twenty minute section of the show. They started with the livestock auction based in Langley. I have always liked them as that is what was next door when I grew up. Pigs, cows, sheep and chickens all take their turn going into the ring as the buyers gather in a semi circle of bleachers choosing what they need to take back to their farm or dinner table. The Indians would buy goats while other ethnic buyers fought over their favourites. Dairy farmers would look to replenish their herd and sell of the young males for beef. There is no smell like a livestock auction as the manure piles up.

The producer wanted to see the real thing, so we showed them how it all worked. The work involved in gathering the goods to sell, setting up a sale, the paperwork involved to make payouts, commission rates everything. They were in my office asking me questions when something triggered me to share some of my testimony. They recorded it and it was broadcast in the middle of the show. I go to proclaim what Jesus had done for me on television that was broadcast all over British Columbia.

They covered two of our major auctions. The first was large estate sale. All our regulars were excited as the cameras would pan over as they bid. Some got to be interviewed and we came out looking good (whew). The second sale was a monster, one of a kind where we liquidated 100's of guns, ammo, gun safes etc from a gun shop that wanted to sell out. We were taking consignments from all over the province. We had some people who wanted to sell pistols, which caused a real uproar in the government offices in Victoria. They had read our advertising and it set of a fire storm. To own or transport a pistol in B.C. you needed a special licence and not many people had one. We had set up a system to cover this problem where the local police would take any sold pistols into their custody until the new buyer could prove that they had a permit to own the pistol. We got a call from the office of the Attorney General of BC telling us that the Minister has issued a cease and desist order, stopping us from selling the pistols. We obeyed. The sale was part of the television program ending with us making a nice profit and a lot of PR. It drove our competitor nuts.

One of the guys who hung around was an old time auctioneer named Larry Brenner. Larry would help, if I needed it. He worked on Wednesdays at the Vancouver car auction as a ring man, making $400 a day. He got me in there as well. I worked for about a year and half. It was fun work with great pay. I got to learn the car business a little and even bought some cars to sell in my auction. I got a broker's license and opened a used car lot near our auction. This added to my enemy's anger and his threats increased. He was winning the war but I sure won some big battles.

Chapter Seven

Bang I'm Broke

By spring 1984 we were in trouble and started to use our overdraft at the bank. We made sure all our consignors were paid, but we couldn't keep up with the mortgage and the loan at the bank. We were falling further and further behind, but I just couldn't quit. Finally two friends came to take me for lunch. They just pointed out the obvious and convinced me to call it quits. I announced it at the next auction. We were done when we sold everything off even the caddy. I bought a junker of a car to get around. We held an auction to sell our house. This was highly unusual at the time and I was real scared as the time approached. I advertised the sale and said to bid they had to bring a $10,000 deposit. Three or four people brought the cashier's checks so we went out on the front steps to hold the sale. We had paid $80,000 and had a $70,000 mortgage to pay off. The bidding was slow but finally two people were serious with the last bid being the exact amount of the mortgage. As I dropped the hammer, I heard a car honk its horn. I turned to see my enemy sitting in his Caddy with a smile on his face while shaking his fist at me. It was a pretty sad day. In the end he and his nephew both died young. The nephew was driving a cube van back to Abbottsford from Vancouver when he took his eyes off the road for a moment and smashed into the back of semi. The uncle died a couple of years later of a heart attack.

It was really hard to admit defeat in the auction business. The pressure was too much for Patsi and she had gone home to get out from under my depression. She came back when the auction closed and the house sold. We packed up our furniture and headed west back to White

Rock, the place that would again become our home. I found a rundown house just up the road from Patsi's parents and we moved in. It was pretty much a dump but the rent was only $400 a month.

I was broke so I borrowed five grand from a friend, at pretty high interest rate and started over. I went back to my old standby, joining the sales team at the same Chrysler dealership where I had bought the pickup. Chrysler had come back from the disaster of the late 1970's under Lee Iacocca's leadership and, in part, by introducing the first minivan. I saw the chance to make some money in a hurry with the popularity of their line. I hit a homerun in my first month with an income of over $5,000. We were on our way back from the deep with this start. I stayed with them as top salesman for the next four months.

It came to an end when Larry, the owner, held a sales meeting. He said that he had been on his way to church on Sunday morning and when he had passed the lot, he noticed several people walking around. He decided that we would be open on Sunday's from then on. Patsi and I had gone back to the church where I attended before and we were committed to it. We were making a lot of new friends and growing in our faith, so I had no intention of missing a service to sell a car. This was in the time before all businesses were open Sundays. Larry went on to say that we all would be all doing Sunday shifts. I responded that I would not be doing that.

It was no surprise that early the next morning the sales manager took me for coffee and let me go. What was the surprise was when Larry called me the next day and offered me the sales manager's job. I think he had looked at his books in the interim and figured out he would be further ahead with me working six days. I turned down the job.

I had used the borrowed money to start buying and selling again. We worked shifts at the car lot so when I didn't have a shift, I was wheeling and dealing. I had signed a non-competitive agreement when I sold CANADA WEST, so I could not open a store until the first of November. I did, however, have a few garage sales and sold things through the newspaper. I sold a lot of the stuff to Larry at the car lot and sold him even more after I was let go. I even sold him my boat and the van.

During our time in Abbotsford, Patsi never saw a doctor. She had a family doctor in White Rock so she booked an appointment soon after we returned. What we found out really put everything into perspective as she had the early signs of cervical cancer. She had minor surgery, which was able to remove all the abnormal cells. If we had not come back to White Rock, she may well have not found it in time. Sometimes God moves in ways we don't understand. What a small price, to lose a business but keep my wife.

Among my new friends at church was Blake Joiner. He and his brother Denis owned Joiner Sales Corp., a large industrial auction company based out of Langley with offices in Calgary and Toronto. Blake is one of the finest men I have ever met. He not only talks of being a Christian, he lives it. He and his wife Adrienne were deeply involved in the church as leaders. Adrienne was the worship leader with a huge classically trained voice. Patsi soon joined the worship team and started to take singing lessons from Adrienne at her home, just around the corner from where we were living.

Patsi has always liked to look her best, with her makeup and dress done perfectly. It was music lesson day and her aunt was going to give her a ride to Adrienne's. As the aunt's van pulled up, Patsi ran out of the house. She swung open the door, jumped into the van, and reached out to close the door. She missed the handle and fell out of the van landing flat on her face in a huge mud puddle. Oh, how I wish I had a camera with me that day. She looked pitiful as her hair drooped down on one side and her face plastered with mud running down to her mouth. Her bright dress was dirty brown with orange highlights. She didn't laugh or cry but just stood there stunned, trying to figure out what had happened. She then ran for the house, never to be seen again. Not quite, but the story carries on these thirty years later.

Blake asked if I wanted to start a Bible study in my home. We invited three other guys and started to meet one morning each week to study "My Utmost For His Highest" by Oswald Chambers I started to read this book as a daily devotional and was awe struck on how pertinent it could be. It seemed that as I would read a day's subject, I would encounter that challenge immediately. It was almost supernatural how a book that was written almost a hundred years before could speak to me so directly. Next to the Bible this book has been the most influential in my life. I still read it every morning, only now from my kindle.

Blake and I became great friends. We had a lot in common, our faith in Christ and our love of the auction business. Blake had started by working with Maynard's auctioneers until he and Dennis struck out on their own. They had worked hard, took calculated risks, and trusted God, who made their business into one of the top industrial auctions in Canada.

As we got to know each other better, they made an offer to be a part of my business restoration. They first lent me the money to pay back the expensive loan. We then had a meeting to discuss how we could partner up to create a new buy/sell business in White Rock. I had the drive to make it happen, while they brought the funding, many contacts in the liquidation business and an especially good standing with the bankruptcy trustees. In the early part of September, 1984 we decided to go ahead

The first thing to do was to form a new company. We needed a name that would stand out while being simple enough to explain what we did. On the side of my auction van I had put the name "PACIFIC COAST AUCTIONS" with a slogan underneath saying "WE PAY CASH-2-U FOR ESTATES AND HOUSEHOLDS". I told the guys that over half the calls I would get would ask if we were that Cash-2-U company so it became a no brainer to call the new company "CASH-2-U FURNITURE LTD". We incorporated the company with Patsi and me owning 50% and Joiner Sales Corp. the other 50%. They put the money into the bank and pretty much set me free.

I found a location in an industrial mall on the edge of White Rock. We could not open for business until the first of November so I worked hard for the next six weeks to fill up the store. I had asked the new owners of 'CANADA WEST CONSIGNMENT SALES" if it would be ok to open a month earlier than the non-competitive agreement said, but they said,

"No way!" They had run the business into the ground during the five years they owned it. That just made my determination to kick butt more real.

They had outright lied to me about the value of the property they had used to pay for the company. The woodlot they had told me was worth $25,000 turned out to be landlocked, surrounded by eight other 100 acre lots owned by her ex-husband. I had to sell it for $5,000 to pay off the bank when we lost the auction.

We opened to great fanfare on the first of Nov. I had been putting teaser ads in the paper for the month of October. Sandwich board signs were painted in bright yellow with red. I had researched the most noticeable colors for signs and these two came out on top. Opening day came with great success. We needed the public's participation not only for sales but to sell us their goods. I was back in a big way.

Patsi and I were working together without too much hassle. Life was good. We stayed in that location for about a year. Canada West closed after only four months, leaving the town to us.

There was a small mall next to the first location for Canada West. It was anchored by a drug store that had been there for over twenty years. The pharmacist owned the mall. He and I had become friends when we were neighbors. I had told him that I wanted to buy the mall whenever he wanted to sell. I got the call, he named a price, and Joiners came up with the money. The deal was made. Joiners owned the mall and I had an option to buy one third for one third of the price they paid.

We moved to the new location in 1986. The store was now in the middle of town, on the main street. Business took another big jump. Patsi and I had moved from the dump of a house to a two bedroom apt near the store. We would have the kids every second weekend. As the kids got older they were more likely to want to stay at home with their friends. Scott would stay with us for a few weeks at a time when he and his mother were at odds.

For the last week of July, 1986 I sent Scott to camp. He had a ball according to the calls I had during the week. He was to come home on Sat. morning. I was waiting for his call to pick him up when the phone rang. It was the manager of the local grocery store. They had caught Scott shoplifting. He had met some guys at camp who told him how easy it was. Scott got caught on his first attempt. I went to the store to get him. He was really shaken up as we headed for the car. I was angry so I thought it best that he run home on his own to think about what he had done. When I went home from work he wasn't there. As the hours grew longer, there was no sign of him. He never made it home. He had spent nights on the street before when he ran away from his mother's, so when he didn't show up I wasn't too worried. I expected him to come home in the morning. He didn't show and I was starting to get real scared. We started to spread the word and I heard from one of his friends that he had spent the night in the local park. I was looking all over for him. I called the police, but no one knew where he was.

The second morning I was desperate when I got word that a friend of mine had seen him the night before, hitching on the freeway that leads to Vancouver. Scott was not quite fourteen and going into Vancouver by himself.

I had to go after him, but how do you find a kid in Vancouver. I started by praying. Cindy was staying with me that weekend so we got on our knees and asked for God's help to find Scott. I left Cindy with Patsi and headed off. I was praying all the way into town. I drove to one of the main streets in Vancouver, parked the car, and started to walk. I didn't have a clue where he could be, but all of a sudden I had a sense of God's leading. I felt a peace that it was all in His hands. I walked until I felt Him say, "Turn right." I turned right. He said, "Go in there." I went in there. I ended up in front of the bus station. He said, "Go in and walk around." I did, but no Scott. I went outside to leave when He said, "Go back and do it again." I did, taking care to look everywhere, still no Scott.

I started to walk towards the stadium. The streets were full of people and the crowds were getting larger the closer I got. This was the long weekend in the summer of 1986. Vancouver was host of the World's Fair and this was the busiest day of the whole six months. As I got to the stadium, I was surrounded by people. This was insane and impossible. There was a small booth with two native guys handing out tracts. I stopped to talk for a second. I told them what I was doing so they prayed with me. I made a donation to their ministry and left. I walked about twenty feet, turned on to a walkway leading towards the fair and Scott walked into my arms. He was there in front of me. I lost it and started to cry in the middle of a hundred people. My son walked into me. It was impossible except there is nothing impossible with God. He heard my prayer. THANK YOU JESUS.

Patsi and I were starting to have problems in the marriage around this time. I was still the screwed up guy from my past in so many ways. I was an out of control "control freak" and that was starting to drive her nuts. Patsi was a stuffer. In her home no one ever expressed their feelings, keeping everything inside. I, on the other hand, was one who had to deal with problems on the spot.I didn't know how to deal with the silent treatment so I didn't have the wisdom to let her have her moods. I would demand that she tell me what was wrong and she didn't know how to do that. Oil and water time began. We didn't know how to change so she kept stuffing and I kept getting mad. It was a recipe for the real trouble which was to come.

I was meeting weekly with a counselor from the church, Dave Anderson. It was helping some. He suggested that I get away for a week by myself to get close to God. Patsi and I discussed it so I booked a trip to Hawaii to sit in the sun and relax. I was to study a book Dave gave me. The subject was Galatians 2:20 - "It is no longer I who lives, but Christ who lives in me." I needed to give up control of my life to Christ. If I kept on living as I had been, I was doomed to lose another marriage.

I boarded a flight out of Vancouver, heading for a condo I had rented from an ad in the Sun. I sat in the middle of the center row of a 747 with no one else in the row. I was feeling a little sorry for myself that I was such a screw up. Patsi didn't want me around and our intimacy was severely lacking. The enemy will seek out areas where we are weak so that's what he did on the plane. There was a beautiful girl in the row ahead who started to talk to me. She was a member of the Australian ski team. When she suggested that she come back and sit with me, I knew it was a recipe for disaster. The body was weak, but the spirit was strong. I had been monogamous since meeting Patsi, by the grace of God, but the temptation was there. I headed for the washroom to get my head straight. On the way back I heard some guys laughing. As I got closer, I overheard one say, "PRAISE THE LORD!" I learned they were going to a Full Gospel Convention in Honolulu. I sat down with them for the rest of the trip. Safe in His arms again.

I checked into my hotel, getting up early to sit by the pool with my book. There was no one at the pool as I stretched in a lounge chair. After a few minutes a bikini clad girl came down. There were thirty or forty chairs, but she came and took the one next to me. I thought – "here we go again" - as she started up a conversation. I lowered my head and asked Him for help again. In about five minutes a couple walked toward the pool. They appeared familiar, but why? They came right up to where I was and said, "Ken, what you are doing here?" It was Eric and Elsie Penner, elders in my church. We hung out together for the next few days, attending the FGBM convention in the evenings. They left for home after four days, leaving Hawaii to me for the last three. My spirit was lifted as I felt Him protect me and work in my life. I was so motivated from being surrounded by believers that I took to doing street evangelism for the rest of the time I was there. I actually got to pray with a young soldier. I had the honor of leading him to the Lord. I was really set free during my time there with the knowledge of how much Jesus loves me. I finally understood that He lives in us. His Spirit shares with our spirit that we are His children. I can do all things in Christ who strengthens me.

On the last day I went to the beach. There were hundreds of good looking girls in skimpy bikinis, but I didn't pay TOO much attention. The day was without a cloud with the temp nearing ninety. I was starting to get a sun burned and had a dilemma. I needed suntan lotion on my back so I finally asked a lifeguard thinking it was sure to be the safest way out. He looked at me and said, "BUGGER OFF YOU QUEER!" I stuttered as I said, "I'm not a a a a ah forget it." I quickly looked for the prettiest girl there and asked for help. She did. I was on a plane home the next day full of faith, hope and a little sunburned.

Our church was at its pinnacle in the mid eighty's. The auditorium was full on most Sundays. Loud enthusiastic worship was always followed by a powerful gospel message. We were a non denominational, spirit filled body where the gifts of the spirit often happened. Prophecy was encouraged and we even invited recognized prophets to minister to the body on special occasions. The leaders had called for one such meeting and the church was full to overflowing. Patsi and I sat off to one side well out of the line of site of the prophets. Those that were selected to be prayed over were set in the first few rows directly in front. A few couples had gone up with the prophets laying hands on them. They gave words of encouragement to each and told them what they felt God wanted them to do in ways of ministries.

After one couple got up they would look down to pick out the next. At this time there seemed to be confusion as they went over to Pastor John and asked a question. After he nodded his head in agreement, they came to the microphone, looked over our way, calling us by name, saying they believed God had a word for us. We were kind of in shock as we went forward. As we went the prophets started to laugh among themselves. They must have known something we didn't. A few of our friends joined in knowing this was going to be good. The laughter grew as we got closer to the stage and by the time we stepped on it, the place was in hysterics. It took a few minutes to calm down and we were soon on our knees with our faces buried in our hands on a chair in front of us, wondering what was happening. The first prophet laid his hand on my shoulder and started to talk. He told me how much I pleased God with my enthusiasm and joy in the house of the Lord. He went on to call me a firecracker and that I would be used by Him. They referred to us as "people of the stuff" causing more laughter because we had warehouses fill with second hand merchandise for the store. Something the prophets would not have known. The three all had wonderful words of encouragement for us both. They told me to keep buying Patsi gifts as that was her love language. Towards the end, one was telling Patsi "Sister, keep the faith, He is going to change, but it will take a long time". That brought the house with Patsi yelling a loud "HALLELUJAH". That was over twenty five years ago and it has come true for the most part. The flesh still occasionally raises its ugly head.

After we had bought the mall, the Joiners offered me an opportunity to own Cash-2-U outright. The company owed them $7,000. They would give me the company outright and forgive the $7,000, if I gave up my option to buy one third of the mall. The mall had increased in value and I didn't have the money to buy my share anyway, so it was a no brainer. The mall turned out to be winner for them and I made our living for the next thirty years from the company.

Property values in White Rock had slumped in the early 80's like everywhere else when interest rates went nuts. By 1987, I could see the values starting to climb up and recognized that if we didn't buy a home now we could be shut out of the market, becoming renters for life. I needed $10,000 for a down payment, but I didn't have it or any real hope of getting it very soon.

I asked the Lord for the money. I believe the bible and trust God for my supply. His word said to ask and believe. He had shown me so often how he looked after us so I trusted Him in this. I had been praying for about a month when I got a call from Blake. He had got a call from a receiver-trustee (an accountant who looks after bankruptcies) asking for a bid on a warehouse full of inventory for hardware stores. The inventory had a wholesale value of $330,000. Blake said they were too busy to do it but, if I wanted to handle it, they would put up the money. We would split the profit. I had two real first-class employees at the store by this time. Karen Batke joined us in late 1985. She became the manager for the next twenty years, being more of a friend then an employee. Patsi often said she was like a second wife to me because it would take two women to raise me. With Karen and Patsi in the store I was able to do outside work.

Blake and I went to see the deal on a Friday morning. It was incredible. We both knew we wanted it the moment we walked thru the door. We could hold a liquidation sale on location and make a strong profit if we bought it right. As we drove home, Blake and I discussed how much to bid. We asked God for help. I got the impression that we should bid twenty two cents on the dollar. I was sure we could sell most of it for fifty cents. It would take about two to three weeks. We would have to pay rent for the warehouse, buy advertising and pay staff. We would net ten to fifteen percent or about thirty to forty thousand, after the dust settled. Blake agreed the numbers were accurate, so he called and made the bid. We heard back in an hour that we had got the deal. I was so excited, I couldn't sleep all weekend. I showed up on Monday morning to take possession.

When I got there I notice some things were missing. Some of the higher end products were no longer on the floor. I then saw a pallet of them over by the loading door. The owners or someone else had removed some of the goods over the weekend. I called Blake and told him the news. He called the trustee who went nuts. He told Blake to make another bid. We decided we would offer eleven cents on the dollar to which the trustee said, "IT IS YOURS!"

Wow! We had the deal in the bag. It was so good now. I called a friend who had a large liquidation store in Vancouver (Ken from Midland Liquidators). I asked him to come over thinking I would sell him a load to start things off. He saw the deal and asked how much for it all. I asked him to make an offer. He called his dad to come over. They talked it over and said they would pay twenty two cents on the dollar. We had just made $33,000 in about an hour. They wrote the check to Joiner Sales. Joiner Sales wrote a check to me for $11,500. We had enough for a down payment on a house. Isn't it great how God works!

Even though I didn't own an auction any more I was still an auctioneer. I got a call from my lawyer friend to sell a pool hall in North Surrey. There were about ten "as new" tables with all the equipment, so we had a real nice crowd. The sale took less than an hour and afterwards Scott and I went for lunch across the road at Wendy's. We ate and were leaving when I got that check in my spirit that God was trying to talk to me. On my right there was a guy sitting by himself. Was I supposed to talk to him? My spirit said yes so I sat down at his table. I said, "I don't know why, but I think God wants me to talk to you." The guy's eyes looked like they were going to jump out of his head. He then tears up as he said that he had rededicated his life to the Lord the night before. He had asked God for a sign that He had heard him. I was the sign. We prayed, thanking the Lord.

We found a new home in Ocean Park that the builder had gone broke on. It needed to be finished. We bought it for $110,000 and paid a friend another $10,000 to finish it. We were back in the real estate market again.

Scott and his mother were having a lot of trouble by now, so we took him in. It always was a problem between Patsi and me. He was my son, not hers, and he was a troubled kid. We were having more problems than just my kids by this time. Patsi finally packed it up and moved in with her sister Sharon who was separated from her husband. It was so serious that we thought we were getting divorced and had both contacted lawyers.

The assistant pastors at the church showed a lot of love and started to work with each of us. John and Lyza Clarke saved us from ourselves. Lyza is the greatest marriage counselor in the world. She was so tough on me, holding me accountable in so many ways. This relationship was to last for the next twenty five years and even to this day her number is on speed dial. I would meet with them and then Patsi would talk with them. One day while I was at home, Patsi showed up. We both broke and cried together. We each forgave each other and agreed to try to do better. That is much easier to say then do, as we would learn over time.

On a call, a man said he was going to sell his home sometime in the future and wanted $75,000 for it. I asked him to call me when he wanted to sell. When he called one day, I wasn't home and Patsi told him we had already bought another house. She told me when I got home and I ran over to his place right away. I didn't have any money so I called Dennis Joiner and he bought it. I wanted to have an option to buy it because it was a two story, brick house with an ocean view. I wanted to live in it. I got an option to buy it for $106,000. The market got real hot around then so we sold the Ocean Park house making about $10,000. We then bought the older house from Denis.

The store was really busy with estates coming in every week. We had a small post office van to pick up the stock. On Saturdays I had extra help, usually two strong young guys with a driver's licenses. They would make pick up, after pick up, all day long, putting the stock on the street all around the store. The store was often so full that we didn't have room for all of the goods. It was almost impossible to handle any more. We would be working until eight pm trying to clear the streets as we piled in the goods, filling the isles that would have to be cleared to open on Monday. We were people of the stuff.

I needed a bigger truck and soon. I had a guy working for us named Dave Greening. Dave was a strong believer so we started to pray. We had a need and sought God's help right away. I was praying at home one morning and God gave me a specific vision of the truck. I saw a white five ton, 1979 Chrysler truck. It was to cost 7,500.00 dollars. I really trusted this vision so I started to look for this specific truck. I called every dealer in Vancouver and surrounding area. One would have the truck, but it was red or another had one, but it was a 1978. They all thought I was nuts and after about two months with the search having moved into Alberta, I started to think so too.

I was getting desperate. On the next Saturday night, we had more furniture than we ever had. Dave and I got on our knees in front of the store, in the midst of it all, and asked God to help and now. On Tuesday morning I picked up the Province and there it was. It matched the description except it was a three ton. I wasn't going to miss it and went off to buy it. It was the right make, color and was 1500 dollars less than I had budgeted. I brought it home and took it to the insurance place. The insurance cost 1500 dollars. The deal, including the insurance, was for the $7500 I had been told.

On a very busy day my brother-in-law Robbie and his friend Kevin were doing the Saturday deliveries. On their first delivery they were to take a very large English wardrobe to a house on the hillside. They loaded it up and set out. A while later they appeared back at the store looking real 'sheepish'. They had parked on the road and climbed up the steep lawn with the wardrobe. Wardrobes are super large and are held together only by corner joints, which make them very fragile. My boys dropped it just before getting to the house. It became firewood and a $400 loss for Cash-2-U. I was peeved, but had to keep my cool, as there was a lot more work to do.

The next stop was for a chest of drawers to be delivered to a brand new condominium bldg. that had opened that day. We got a telephone call from the manager that my guys were able to drop the dresser on the new marble floor in the entryway, breaking a tile. Another $300 hit. When they got back I was beside myself. Patsi and Karen were in fear for the guys. They came in together and stood in front of me. I lost my control of my mouth for a minute and out came a now infamous statement, "IF I HAD WANTED TO HIRE A**HOLES, I WOULD HAVE ADVERTISED FOR A**HOLES." The girls went into hysterics, laughing so hard they peed their pants. As they lost it, the boys lost their jobs and I lost $700.

Over the years I must have had over 100 different people for work us. I had three long-term employees who I could trust with every aspect of the business. Karen started first and stayed the longest. I needed a guy whom I could train to buy/sell so when Hal Marriott showed up with a great resume and, better still, a reference from one of my best friends, we struck a deal. Hal became my right hand for the next three years until he wanted to set out on his own. After Hal left, Dolly Titus joined Karen for fifteen years. Oh, what I put them through.

I would often hire guys off the street who came looking for handouts. I have to admit it usually backfired but never quite as bad as with this little French man named Arman. He showed up with another guy whose aunt was a friend of Pastor Vern. I put them on pickups and deliveries. Arman had no teeth and was about five ft tall.

There was a six day auction in Seattle that was liquidating a national wholesaler. It was similar to the one we did in Vancouver, but this one was about ten times bigger and full of high end inventory. I went down and was spending a ton of money. I was in for about $15,000 and wanted to buy a lot more. I called the bank and they gave me a line of credit over the phone. I was in for around $25,000 when the dust settled. The truck was being used for deliveries while I was away so I came home to get it. Arman and I headed down, loaded it, and headed back, knowing we would have to go back the next day to get the rest. We had unloaded about a third of the truck by eight pm and were exhausted so we quit for the day, with the intent to finish in the morning. I had a cheap motion detector alarm in the store that would call the police with a taped message. I locked the truck up and parked it across the street from the store, hanging the keys on the wall. When I came back with Arman the next morning, the truck was gone. The side door of the store was wide open and the alarm had been turned off. I called and the police who were there in an instant. A new sofa set and some leather coats were missing as well as about $10,000 worth of the new inventory still in the truck. I was sick to my stomach but I had to go back to Seattle to get the rest of the stuff so I rented another truck.

I was just heading out when the police called. They had found our truck. Of course it had been cleaned out. I had insurance but was worried that the stuff in the truck would be covered. I found out that if the truck was parked was within fifty ft. of the store, I was insured. If it was over, I was out of luck. The street was about thirty ft wide so I was OK by ten ft. As the police investigation moved forward the main suspect was my man Arman. I guess his past led them to suspect him. If you added it up, it had to be him because the alarm had been turned off and he was the only one who knew what was in the truck. I wish I had learned that lesson better but similar things happened twice more over the years. The insurance covered the loss after I paid the thousand dollar deductible.

Chapter Eight

What The Counseller Found Out

Patsi and I were doing a lot of counseling with Lyza. It came out that Patsi was really angry with me in a lot of ways. Because of my upbringing I was unable to really express love. I really didn't know what love was, let alone how to express it.

We would meet with Lyza about once a week, so I was in the middle of these two women who were beating the crap out of me. I needed to hear it, but I would become defensive after I felt I was hearing too much. It turned out that one of the major problems was that Patsi felt I had robbed of having the wedding of her dreams. She always envisioned the big wedding with her father walking her down the aisle as she wore her white dress; her sisters as her bride's maids and the big reception.

In one of my meetings with Lyza, I came up with the idea that we should pull off a surprise wedding for Patsi. Lyza had never heard of such a thing. How could it be possible? She had to admit it would be "off the wall" to express my love for Patsi in this way. She didn't think it could be done, so we decided to try something. If we could find a way for Patsi to try on a wedding dress, without telling her why, Lyza would accept that as a sign from God that we could do it.

We had to find a way to solve this problem. The scam began with a story that Lyza's daughter, Julie, needed a pair of white gloves that were only available at a wedding store. On one of their days together she and Patsi stopped by the store to get the gloves. I had called the lady at the store the day before and told her the story. She thought it was the greatest thing she had ever heard of.

The girls arrived at the store to get the gloves and the store was empty. There were all these beautiful dresses all over the place. Lyza told a "white lie" saying to the lady that she had never got to wear a white dress at her wedding. The lady then said, "Well, go ahead now. There is no one here so have some fun." Lyza played her part to a tee and started to try on dresses. She told Patsi to do it too, but Patsi didn't want to play. After Lyza's third dress, Patsi finally gave in and grabbed a dress and went into the change room. The saleslady was a pro, so when Patsi came out she said, "As nice as that one looks, you should try this one." Patsi resisted, telling her "YOU KNOW WE ARE BOTH MARRIED AND AREN'T BUYING ANYTHING." The lady laughed and said she was having as much fun as the girls. The second dress looked super on her. The lady started to grabbing quick handfuls of fabric, getting as close to a measurement as possible without Patsi catching on..

We did it. We had a dress, so it was all systems go. Lyza and I planned the wedding for January twenty fourth, which would be our 5th anniversary. John would do the service. I got the pastor that married us, Ken Gretter, to stand up for me as a groomsman and Blake Joiner would be my Best Man. Both Patsi sisters were Maids of Honor. I booked a room for a reception in a restaurant that would cater the meal. We had a florist in the church look after the flowers. We had a bluegrass band from the church. And I booked a suite in a high-end hotel overlooking the water in Vancouver for our wedding night. Most everyone in the church knew what was up, but Patsi was kept in the dark. Patsi's family thought it was impossible, but somehow we kept it a secret.

On the big day we had arranged to go out for dinner with John and Lyza. We went to pick them up at the church. Lyza came out to the car and asked Patsi to come in to see the decorations they had worked on for the woman's meeting the next day. She led her to the smaller sanctuary with two swinging doors that were closed. The room was dark. As the doors were open and Lyza led Patsi in all of a sudden the lights were turned on and Patsi was standing in the middle of her wedding with her father and mother standing just in front to meet her. She was asking what was this and Lyza told her, "THIS IS YOUR WEDDING!" Over a hundred friends and relatives were there, cheering and crying. Patsi broke down. Her sisters came and took her out of the room.

They took her into an office where she saw her wedding dress. There was jewelry, shoes, and a beautiful hat. Everything she needed. After a half hour or so, all was ready and she got to walk down the aisle on her father's arm.

The reception was wonderful except I had forgotten to set seats for my friends in the band. They were giving me a complimentary evening of music and I forgot to feed them! We solved it in a hurry and they forgave me.

Patsi and I went off for a wonderful time in a beautiful room. We were able to share our love for each other without a lot of the garbage that had been between us. She knew I loved her and she had so much more grace for me. We would need it and a lot more in the years to come.

I had not only planned the wedding, with Lyza's help, but had booked a honeymoon in Mexico. I went to local travel agency who suggested Puerto Vallarta. We looked up all the offers from the brochures and decided the best deal was at a resort called Arthur's and Poncho's. We were to leave two days after the wedding, to give Patsi a chance to pack. The flight down was smooth as was the landing, which was much to Patsi's relief. As we got off the plane to clear customs, we came face to face with Mexico. The airport was in an open sided aluminum shed with customs and many police carrying machine guns. It made you stand up straight and answer any questions very clearly. We got through and saw an open sided bus with a sign showing the name of our resort. We boarded and headed out with about twenty other people. In the distance we could see the crystal blue of the Pacific with waves sparkling as they came ashore. You could see the wide paths of sand beach that ran for miles. Excitement reigned as we moved closer to paradise. Then our bus made a sharp left, heading away from the sea and drove into the desert. What was happening? Where were we going? We just went deeper and deeper into the sand until we came upon a huge white adobe wall. Where was the ocean I had seen in the brochure? The bus pulled up to the lone entrance, a hole in the wall, and our spirits sunk. What had I done, this was supposed to be one of the best times in our lives and now what?

I didn't say a word as I took our bags and followed the others thru the hole. We entered an atrium that looked like it was out of the movies. All was not lost after all. There were huge palm trees reaching up to the fifty ft shade covering roof. Many multi colored birds were perching on pedestals with tropical flowers lighting up the atmosphere. Off in the distance I could see the pools that we shown so prominently in the brochure. There were three with in water bars at each one. I could see a smile on Patsi's face as we waited to check in. Our turn came and we received a key for a room on the third floor. We were directed to the elevator located in another bldg. along a pathway, next to a manicured lawn. As we made our way I was noticing there was no one in the pools. I wondered why? We continued until we reached the door of the elevator. Trouble raised its head when Patsi saw that it was covered with graffiti. Are you kidding me? Down went the feelings and they hit bottom when the elevator literally crashed and banged its way to the third floor. It would hit one side and rebound over see how hard it could hit the other. Patsi hates elevators at the best of times, so she was almost sick when it came to a stop, but not before it bounced up and down as if it was on a bungee cord, finally slowing enough for the door to open. We had to step up about four inches to get on the floor. I was nervous too but didn't dare let her know.

We dragged our luggage off this amusement ride towards our room. I had the lone key so I turned the lock and swung the door inwards. I grabbed the two cases and walked toward the bed to throw them on top. I raised the cases high in the air just as I got to the edge when I fell headfirst onto the bed. I tripped over a slab of cement on the floor. There was no box spring, just this slab of cement sticking out about six inches from a thin mattress that was thrown on top. I scraped my legs as I fell. This was bad and getting worse by the second. With every ounce of strength I had, I smiled at Patsi and said, "It seems comfortable." I LIED RIGHT TO HER FACE!

I had to escape her presence so I went into the bathroom. As I went to wash my hands, I was tested again. There was no water. As I twisted and turned the handles, I sensed I was being watched. I looked up to see a large green gecko that had decided to stick his head out from behind the mirror, looking me straight in the eye. This is crazy! I lost it and said, "WE HAVE TO GET OUT OF HERE NOW!"

I threw our luggage back to the box that was held up by a rope, put our lives at risk once more and made the trip back down to the front desk. The poor girl had to deal with Patsi being close to hysterics and with my anger. We demanded that this had to end and end fast. She gave us a ground floor room next to the pool. It was a much larger room with a door opening to the pool area. The fact that there was a two inch space between the top of the door and the door frame didn't bother us at the time. The relief of not having to ride the suicide elevator again was enough. It had running water. We didn't even notice the cement slab

The confusion and stress was getting to be too much for Patsi and we had only been in Mexico for two hours. I knew we had to get out of this place, if only for the evening. I called a cab to take us downtown. The "Smiling Mexican" (that was his name, perhaps because he had no teeth) drove us like he was escaping from jail. Maybe he was. He drove through every color of light without slowing down. The roads were like a roller coaster with the cab lifting off the road at the top and crashing to the ground as we entered the valley at the bottom. Patsi started to cry as she clung to the back of the front seat. There were no seat belts so we were free to be tossed to and fro with us both hitting our heads on the roof twice. By now all I had done had been lost in the first three hours in Mexico. We were in hell and had to survive.

I paid the cab and got out. I knew I was in trouble when Patsi got out the other door and slammed it so hard it almost came off. The driver looked at her and decided it was safer to drive away than to confront her. I, on the other hand, lacked that wisdom. Patsi went into a shell. Just like a turtle. She wasn't really there, just her body. We were next to one of the most beautiful beaches in the world, so I started to walk on the beach hoping the serenity would calm her down. Not to be. She followed me at a distance. I would walk and she followed about fifty feet behind me. I would stop and so would she. This went on for about fifteen minutes. Off in the distance, I could hear mariachi music that grew louder as we walked along. I finally got up to where it was coming from, so I headed off the beach towards the music. Patsi closed up but still wouldn't walk with me.

I reached the building in about thirty steps. It was a two level and there was party happening on the second story, so up the stairs I went. Patsi was at my heels by now, not that she wanted to, but she was too frightened to be alone. The party was in full swing as we sat down. There were waiters passing out margaritas, tequila shots, and Corona beer, so I quickly had one of each. We were sitting with a young couple from Canada. They were pretty happy that we sat down with them. It turned out the party was for people who had bought timeshare memberships that day. I HATE TIMESHARES. The company who was putting on this party was getting everyone hammered so that they wouldn't back out of their deal. The booze was flowing free so I had a little too much, well maybe a lot too much. Patsi started to loosen up a little so that after three hours, when my new best friends decided we should all go down to Carlos O'Brian's, the world famous party bar, we said, "Of course!" Well, I said that. I was so far gone that I don't know what Patsi said. We spent the next few hours dancing on the tables and singing at the top of our lungs. Patsi had a few drinks, just enough to be able to take the cab ride home. The next morning I was sicker than I ever had been in all my life. They served us cold fried eggs for breakfast. I went from blue to green and ran to the room.

We sat around the pool for most of the day while I felt sorry for myself, making many promises that that it would never happen again. Another couple, who had been on our bus to the resort, were sitting next to us. We got talking and I told them our story from the night before. I soon learned that I was talking to the president of the North Vancouver AA. Andy McGregor had been sober for a number of years and believed his role was now to get me off the booze. It didn't matter that I didn't drink that often, it was the fact that I got hammered that intrigued him. I never had another drink on that trip, thanks to Andy. We spent the next two weeks together. We would spend most days at the beach basking in the glorious sunshine. Each day I watched as the parasailors were lifted high in the sky to sail around the inlet on their parachutes before they gently floated down to land on their feet back on the floating dock. After the third day watching this tranquil sport, I decided it was my turn. I walked over to the booth and laid my money down. A young boy led me thru the water to climb upon the float. It was rocking in the waves but that didn't bother me and I was soon strapped in this heavy harness. It had many metal, fist size clamps to lock you in and must have weighed over forty lbs. I knew what was to happen from watching for the last two days. The boat slowly pulls ahead until the rope to the harness is tight. The driver then hits the power, the parachute fills with air and you are lifted into the heavens. That is how it is suppose to work. But when it was my turn, the boat that was powered by twin, 150 hp Mercury's, has one of its motors sputter and quit, just as I hit the water. There was not enough power to lift me up so I started to be dragged behind. Now, because I had all this weight from the harness on, I started to act like a fisherman's downrigger, sinking at a forty-five degree angle. With each second I dove deeper and deeper. The fish all were staring at this fat white whale as it dragged by. Then, just as I was about to hit bottom, the other motor ignited, increasing the speed that filled the parachute and I exploded out of the water like a 200 lb cork. People on the beach must of thought it was the rapture. Halleluiah!!!!

One day, as the four of us strolled the streets, we found a hole in the wall restaurant that served fresh seafood. We noticed that the picnic tables were filed with locals so we entered. With some trepidation I ordered the blackened snapper. It was served whole on a large platter size plate. It appeared from the back kitchen looking as if it had come from a four star restaurant. It was laid out flat, filling the plate, like it was a flounder with two eyes staring up at you as you cut into it. I was in heaven at the first bite. Without a doubt it was the most delicious fish I had ever tasted. Spicy and moist, crispy skin covering the sweet flesh, it was incredible. I ate it every day for the last few days of our holiday. Vancouver has world-class restaurants, but I think that hole in the wall served the best fish ever.

Andy saw his role as my protector, preaching AA doctrine to me daily. I preached Jesus. We didn't do it over beer, just coffee and pop. At the end of the two weeks Andy had received Jesus and I stayed sober. I occasionally take drink now and then but never like I did that night in Mexico. We got together with Andy and his lady at our home in White Rock to reminisce a while later. Denny Boyd was a columnist for the Vancouver Sun for many years and a man for whom alcohol was an enemy that almost destroyed him. Andy met Denny thru AA and they became lifelong best friends. Andy was often mentioned in his columns as MC'EYEBROWS.

Along with many pictures and memories, Patsi brought home a parasite from eating a hot dog served from a vendor on the beach. That was a big mistake, making her sick for the next two months. We didn't go back to Mexico for many, many years. She always says that was the only holiday where she lost weight.

Patsi's dad, Art had two heart attacks later that year. He was a heavy smoker and also a diabetic. His first happened in April with the second in August. They performed an operation for a special kind of dialysis because his kidneys had failed. He was a very sick man.

He never showed any interest in religion. He had seen how much I had changed over the years, but he knew me as a fanatic from the exuberance I had at the beginning. I had tried to share Jesus with him many times, but it was without success. I knew we had a limited time left and so we were praying everyday for him.

One day he was having a real bad time, so Pastor Vern and I went to his house to pray over him. Art said he was having the "heebee jeebee's". That was his description of having some kind of nervous breakdown. He was struggling to deal with everything that was happening to him in a short period of time. We laid hands on him and he calmed down in a few moments. It was the first time he experienced the power of prayer.

He went into Peace Arch Hospital in August and was placed in the ICU. I was there one day when he was having the "heebie-jeebies" again, so I laid my hand on his forehead and asked for God's peace to come over him. He calmed immediately and told Norma, after I left, that if he got out of there, they would have to start going to church.

Patsi and I prayed for her dad daily. One day in late September I felt the Lord say that today was the day to share with him again, so I went to the hospital to tell him that today was the day God wanted him to surrender. I shared the gospel and ended by asking him if he wanted to receive Jesus as his Savior. He said yes and we prayed. Norma was also there and to my surprise, she prayed and asked Jesus into her life at the same time.

Patsi and I needed a break so we got ready for a holiday. A few years before I had found a small motel in Palm Desert that was fantastic. It was left over from the 1920's, looking like nothing from the outside, but when you entered into the courtyard you were met by brightly lit palm trees, a beautiful manicured lawn centered by a large heated pool with lounge chairs all around under shade umbrellas. In one corner was a hot tub, which became my "favorite" spot, especially at night when you could sit and watch the stars and enjoy a glass of wine. It was a paradise. It became our retreat for the next few years. In late November, we packed to spend three weeks there.

We spent most days at the pool. I would play golf a few times as Patsi got to shop. On one occasion I lost a ball in a large swampy, reed filled area on the edge of a fairway. I dove in to retrieve my ball where I found myself in golf ball heaven. I was soon gathering several quality balls, most from under the water, when a course marshal came up and asked if I was not afraid of the snakes that lived there. I leaped out of the swamp like a gazelle. I didn't stop shaking for at least twenty minutes.

There was a huge weekly flea market set up at the local college. It was like many markets today with most vendors offering new items at discount prices. There was one booth that really intrigued me. The guy was selling beautiful, machine made carpets for ridiculously low prices. They were selling like crazy. They were in all sizes from doormat size up to some that would fill a room, in many different patterns and colors. I asked how he did it. He was quite forthright telling me that they were all factory seconds. He told me more and more until I had learned that he had worked for a carpet factory in Bruge, Belgium. He would go over once a year and buy a container load. I kept asking questions and he kept answering them. By the end, I knew who, what, where, and how much. I went back to the hotel and made contact with the factory. They had lots of product and said there were many factories in the surrounding area, so that a load would be no problem. I decided I would go to Belgium as soon as I got home.

We had to be home for Christmas, so we started heading north on the morning of the 17th December, We travelled a long day, covering about 600 miles before we checked into a motel for the night. Patsi called her mom to see how her dad was. To her surprise, he was at home for a visit from Vancouver General where he had been moved to from Peach Arch, in White Rock. She got to talk for a few minutes and tell him how much she loved him. We hit the road in the morning arriving home around eight pm.

Patsi went to her mom's right away while I stayed home to unpack. As she walked into her parents' home the telephone rang. Patsi answered and heard the person ask for Norma. Norma and Sharon had just gotten home from driving Art back to the hospital. Norma took the phone to hear the doctor say that Art had just passed away. The McKay family went into shock. I took a cab to the house as fast as I could. I arrived as many other relatives and friends began to show up to console Norma. Patsi has this ability to deal with difficult situations whenever they happen, saving her breakdown until later so she handled the situation, taking charge.

As the family gathered, we all sat around in shock. Daughters and sister-in-laws sat comforting Norma. Life without Art would be difficult for Norma and the girls. He was their rock. The first call from the doctor was soon followed with a request to donated organs. In their grief they caught the vision of helping a stranger. It created a way for Art's body to live on. They agreed that Art would have wanted it to be. Someone, somewhere has vision because of their decision. I helped to organize the cremation, the government death benefit and the celebration of life, where I got to share how God must have needed some more golden highways made, so he brought Art, "The best bulldozer operator in the world", home to take charge. We also told of Art's conversion. A lot of tough men got to hear the truth that day. Patsi often talks about how strange it was to see the world just keep moving on. She wanted to yell, "DON'T YOU KNOW MY FATHER JUST DIED!"

It was such a blessing that we had had the wedding earlier that year and Patsi got to walk down the aisle on his arm.

Chapter Nine

The Business Is Rockin' – I Get Rocked

The store was running well under Karen's guidance. I decided to go to Belgium for a load of carpets, booking tickets for a friend and myself to Amsterdam, after making arrangements for a letter of credit from the bank. Tickets were about half price by booking a seven day trip from Seattle to Amsterdam. My friend Ross, who was married to Patsi's cousin Debbie, and I were full of anticipation as we headed out. We were to fly on a 747 with over 400 other passengers. In the waiting room were people of every shape and color. Most were dressed casually as we were to be in the air for over nine hours on our way over the North Pole. There was one person who was unlike any other. This girl was tall, wearing the tightest top and the shortest mini skirt ever. She had a cute face, but no one noticed. We boarded in order by sections with Ross and I sitting in the middle row with five others. There was one seat left next to me. We were ready to depart when guess who trots down the aisle to sit next to me. Legs and boobs everywhere as she squashed in beside me. I just laughed. All those young single guys and she plunks down next to me. I said hello and learned it was going to be a long flight. She was a silly girl with a high-pitched nasal voice. I learned she wanted to be an actress. I wonder if it ever happened.

After we landed in Amsterdam, we picked up a rental car and hit the freeway, Belgium bound. We located a hotel near Bruge and crashed, waking up totally suffering from jetlag. After a couple of hours of searching we found the factory. After introductions we were taken to a huge room full of factory seconds. You had to look at each carpet, deciding if you wanted it or not. Some had very slight flaws, a missed stitch or a slight dye error. Others had major holes and were unsalable. They left us alone all day as we picked out the best. I bought enough to fill a twenty foot container. After we had finished we had to decide where to go as we had six days to kill. We headed east into France, spending the next few days in Paris. We visited all the famous landmarks. We went up to the top of the Eiffel tower, down to stare at Mona Lisa in the Louvre. We stayed on the right side of the left bank, next the bridge beside Notre Dame, while making the most of each day. From sitting in a small café eating cheese and croissants while watching people walk by to going to the International Air Show the day after a Russian Mig crashed during a demonstration of a vertical flight using the afterburner. I always enjoyed Europe since my time there in the sixties but Ross fell in love with it and has taken Debbie and his sons back many times since.

We got back, with the carpets following about six weeks later after crossing the Atlantic, traversing the Panama Cannel and coming up the west coast. I got the newspaper to cover the arrival when I told the story of how they came to be coming to White Rock. We rented a separate store for the carpets and hired a young salesman. They sold like mad and I was soon on the phone arranging to get another load. I took Patsi this time and after we bought the carpets, I took her to see the part of Germany where I had been posted. She hated the old buildings and was always on the lookout for a Holiday Inn. We got through Germany with her only having one breakdown. I got to go back to my old army base; reliving many of the memories.

The bar we had bombed was still there, under new management. I decided Holland would be more to her liking. Not the part where I used to go but some of the small villages. I was right and we had a nice few days in Rotterdam. The Dutch treated us like family. It was a great time.

We stayed in Amsterdam for final night to be near the airport. The flight home was booked for eight am so we got up at four to be at the airport by six. The plane was delayed eight hours so that we didn't leave until four pm. We both were a little grumpy when we finally boarded but got a lot more so when after six hrs in the air they informed us that Seattle was socked in and we would be landing in San Francisco. We spent the next few hours on hard seats, staring out the windows before finally getting off the plane in Seattle, twenty four hours after we woke up.

This time the carpets took a little longer to sell, but they were still very profitable. I went by myself the last time spending my extra days at the Brussels auto show, the largest in Europe, before heading home. I arrived in Amsterdam to return to Seattle. The flight was on time, but I took my time to board as I usually do when I know I am going to be stuck in a seat for hours. I was one of the last to board. I reached up to put my bag in the overhead, when a suited man addressed me, "Mr. Metherel?" I said, "Yes?" He asked me to please come with him. I said, "Just a moment." as I put my bag up. He said for me to bring the bag with me. What was going on?

I followed him out to where there were four other guys, all in suits. They said they were from Interpol and was my name Ken Metherel. I said, "Yes?" thinking there must be someone else in the world with my name. They then asked if I lived in Surrey, BC. As I replied in the affirmative, I knew I was in trouble. They asked me many questions about where I had been and what had I been doing. They had a picture of a man that wasn't me. This guy somehow had gotten my I.D. and was using it as he committed crimes. They finally let me go back onboard. As I headed for my seat the stewardess directed me to another seat, as they had given mine away, thinking I wouldn't be back. They put me next to a little lady in a seat next to the door where I had been interviewed. She had overheard all the conversation. I had to laugh as she almost puked when I sat down. I have not been back to Europe since.

The business was doing well and the real estate market was moving forward too. We had sold the duplex lot for a profit and so we were in a good financial position. I was doing a call on 176th St., two miles east of White Rock. As I heading back to the store I saw an open house sign on a small acreage. I don't know what drew me, but in I went. It was a three and a half acre horse farm with a 3000 sq. ft. home. The land was all fenced with a seven stall, two story barn and a machine shed. The asking price was $300,000. I tooled around the place and talked to the agent for awhile, saying that I thought real estate was in for a correction in the near future and when it got to 225 k. I would be a buyer. To my surprise the agent called the next day and said we might have a deal. I convinced Patsi that we should go see it. She agreed with me after the viewing so we were ready to make an offer. The realtor came to my home the next day and we wrote an offer of $225,000 with fifty thousand down and asked that the vendor to take back a mortgage of the balance for two years at ten percent (the going rate at that time). We were excited as we waited to hear back. The next day we met with the agent who presented a counter offer. The price went from 225k to 250k but the best part was that they would give the mortgage for 200k without any interest for two years. A quick calculation showed that interest payments for two years on the 175k would have added up to $37,500. So with the increase of $25,000 and the saving of $37,500 we were now buying the place for $12,500 less than our first offer. Wow what a great deal. We quickly signed and then listed our house, which sold in less than a week.

We moved in about sixty days later with Norma taking a bedroom at the end of the house. She was left in a tough financial situation after Art died. To create some income she rented out her home and moved in with us. It worked well as I travelled a lot and Patsi would now always have someone to keep her company.

After we settled in, we bought three horses. "Of course" we needed all the tack and were soon out a few thousand bucks. I enjoyed the horses, riding around the area looking like a bounty hunter. A large western hat and a heavy rainproof slicker were my daily wear. It was fun training the third horse, a young Arab male. It was especially neat to see Patsi out in the training area with a 30ft lead and whip in her hand. It soon proved that we were out of our league. We sold the horses after about six months.

I learned that the property taxes were going to be ridiculous. The answer was to use the land as a farm, qualifying for farm taxes, about twenty five percent of the residential rates. The most popular method was to raise cattle for a few months each year, buying them in the spring, feeding them the grass and sell them off in the fall. I had been given a warning that to qualify for the next tax year I had to move quickly.

Off to Fraser Valley Livestock Auctions, where I went crazy. I bought up all these calves that had just been weaned from their mothers that day. I had seventeen of them delivered a couple of hours later. I had running water in the front field ready for them to graze in. We watched our new herd for a while then off to bed.

After two days my neighbor came over to ask us for our help. Our home was at the back of the property with the field with the calves at the front. Our neighbor's house was up by the road with their bedroom next to the field with the calves. The calves were gathering outside their bedroom window and crying for their mothers all night long. They had gone two nights without sleep and couldn't stand it anymore. We opened the gate, letting the calves back into a larger part of the farm. Fortunately for us the crying soon went away as they were now near our bedroom.

Life as a cattle farm had lots of pitfalls. They would break down the fences and escape all over the neighborhood. They all had to have shots at regular intervals so I became the vet to save money. There is a video of me chasing a calf around a pen with a needle in my hand. Once I got it in, the calf took off with the needle bouncing from side to side until it finally fell to the ground.

On another occasion I had kept one calf in a pen and was feeding it a lot of extra grain to fatten it up, before having it butchered for our freezer. My brother-in-law Robbie was hired to clean the manure from the stall. The smell was too much for him and he said he couldn't do the job. I went to a second hand store and found a gas mask for him. He went back to work, telling me how much better it was with the mask. Again we have pictures of this guy shoveling manure with this mask covering his face. A real sight! The story is even better because I found out later he didn't close the vents on the mask so he was breathing exactly the same smell as before only now with a sweaty rubber mask on. Too funny!

The cattle became expensive to feed because we had to buy loads of grain from the co-op, because we ran out of grass. As the calves grew they were starting to destroy the fields. The farm had become a mud pit with the cattle walking everywhere in about a foot of mud. The cattle business ended when Patsi and I wanted to go to Palm Springs for a holiday. I called the auction and they rounded up the herd. We sold them for a small profit, but it sure was a lot more work than it was worth. We did get the tax break.

I was now buying loads of products from a warehouse in Los Angeles. It was excess goods for the 99 Cent stores. A truckload was very profitable since Canadian prices were so much higher than American. On one of my loads, I bought a pallet of Mexican beer for $50.00. That was about the cost of a case here. On the way home, as I went over the scale as I entered Oregon, I was 300 lbs. overweight. I either had to lose the weight or pay $400 for a permit to carry the extra weight. I got a brainwave and pulled ahead into the parking lot. I made a sign for the truckers offering cases of beer for five dollars. I lost the 300 lbs. in less than an hour and had a fist full of cash.

To haul the loads, I had bought a 5th wheel cargo trailer that had been used by Frito Lay in Bellingham. It was all aluminum and made by Grumman, the aircraft manufacturer. I bought a new Chevy one-ton dually to pull it. I would go back and forth from Los Angeles three or four times a year. On one of the trips I saw a yard in a Los Angeles suburb with a few of the same trailers. I stopped to talk with the owner and found out that Frito Lay was selling all the trucks and trailers from their facility in Ontario, California. I was constantly bombarded with guys who wanted to buy my trailer. They had been used to haul chips, etc. so they had no wear on them. There were about twenty for sale when I got there. I bought a truck and trailer for $3,000 with a promise to buy many more. I took my dually home with a load and flew back for the new one. They were powered with a small v8. It was lots of power for their intended use but lacking for hauling loads from California to Canada. I got the first one home without much hassle. I had it sold for $10,000, within a week.

I booked the next flight to get number two. This time I had some breakdowns. The load I had was far too heavy for the motor especially climbing the mountains along Hwy 5. It would overheat so I would have to stop to let it cool down and fill it with water before I could set out again. It took three long days of driving to make it. The units would sell almost as fast as I could get them back so I was going back and forth as often as I could.

On the next trip, just as I arrived at my hotel, Scott called to say pastor Vern had died. What a shock. I got up early, headed for the Frito Lay yard, picking up my unit. I loaded as fast as possible from the warehouse in downtown LA, hitting hwy 5, northbound. I had the normal trouble so that I had no extra time because the funeral was on Thurs. morning. I got to the border with about three hours to spare. Vern meant so much to me. I had lost a very good friend as well as my pastor.

The next two trips were to be the last. The second to last trip had its breakdown as I started up the grapevine about a 100 miles north of LA. I started to smell smoke and so I pulled off the highway. As I lifted the hood, flames broke out. I wasn't smart enough to have a fire extinguisher so I sat and watched the fire spread. It, fortunately, was confined to the motor area as there was nothing to burn to allow it to spread to the cargo. After a couple of minutes one of the radiator hoses burned through, causing the water to explode, putting out the fire.

A tow truck showed up in under an hour. We unhooked the trailer, leaving it locked on the side of the highway while the cab and I went back down the hill to the town. We left the cab at a truck repair service that was closed, as it was around ten pm.

I grabbed my bag and headed to find a motel. I stopped at the local truck stop. When I went to the washroom, I saw that I was black, covered in suit from the fire. I cleaned up a little but was still a mess. There were no rooms at the truck stop. The guy behind the counter told me there were two motels in town, so I headed out to find them. The first also had no rooms. I found the other, only to hear the same story. The clerk was a nice kid who was truly sorry but there was nothing he could do. I had nowhere to go so we stated to talk. He was a Christian and I soon was telling him the whole deal, including how God had talked to me. He was amazed and we ended up praying together. I told him I was going to find the local park to sleep under a tree. I left, but decided to go back to the truck stop to see if I could find a chair to sleep in before I looked for the park. As I walked into the truck stop the tel. rang. The clerk answered it, looked at me as I walked in, and said, "IT'S FOR YOU."

It was the clerk at the hotel. He said that a couple had checked out of their room and I could have it. I went from having to sleep under a tree to a queen size bed. The Lord was looking after me again. The repair shop rewired the truck after I got the OK from ICBC insurance, which paid the bill. I was on the road by the next evening.

The trip was uneventful until I was about forty miles south of Olympia, WA. The trailers were tandem axles and could handle most loads. The problem was that on this unit the tires were showing more wear than normal. I had a blowout on the right rear. I didn't have spares for the trailers or a jack that could lift it so I would have to wait for another tow truck. I sat by the side of the road for a couple of minutes before I decided to poke along real slow until I got to the next exit, to reach a safer place to have the truck worked on.

It took about an hour to go fifteen miles, driving real slow, keeping the load off the rim. I turned off the freeway and headed towards a restaurant with a huge parking lot on the west side of the hwy. It was about five pm when I went into to use the phone to call the tow company. I ate dinner and waited, and waited, and I waited some more. I was getting more frustrated by the minute. It was about eight thirty before the tow truck driver pulled up.

He took a look at the situation and told me that there is a service station down the road where I could buy a used tire. He took the tire off, tossed it in the back, and we headed south. We just got on the freeway when I sense the Lord say I want this one. I knew His voice so I looked for an opening. This was just after Jimmy Swaggart had his big fall and so that is what I used to open him up. I asked what he thought about Swaggart and the floodgate opened. He dumped everything he had against Christians. Every Christian failing was brought out…hypocrites, liars, cheats, money grabbers... Every sin was mentioned until he seemed to run out of things to say and his anger slowed down. I asked if there was more. He didn't reply, so I said, "AREN'T YOU GLAD JESUS ISN'T LIKE THAT?" He was stunned. I shared my story how I had felt exactly like he did and what God did for me. This was a divine appointment. He softened up so I asked if he wanted to ask Jesus into his life. He said his wife had been praying for him for years. Two big old boys held hands with tears running down our faces as he came to the Lord. It was so amazing. We fixed the tire and I drove off after a hug. I was so much at peace, as I made my way home. It was another example of how God works all things for his glory. If I hadn't had the flat where I did, when I did, if he hadn't been so busy to cause him to be so late… Everything was of the Lord.

This story has an even better follow up. I was heading to L.A. with an empty trailer about a year later. I got to Olympia for dinner and after I came back to the truck I had a flat. I headed for the service station where we had bought the tire the year before. When I arrived I asked about the tow truck driver. The guy behind the counter said, "OH, YOU MEAN JOHN. HE GOT RELIGION ABOUT A YEAR AGO AND IS OFF IN THE MISSION FIELD WITH HIS FAMILY." I guess the guy wondered why I was rubbing my eyes as I walked out the door. I sure look forward to seeing John in heaven.

I was so charged up from this I could hardly drive. I had made it to Roseburg, in central Oregon, by noon the next day, when it started to pour. I needed new wiper blades and so I pulled into a truck service yard. The guy took me in right away and in ten minutes I was ready to go. I had driven into the bay so he had to direct me as I backed out with the big trailer. As I was ready to leave I asked if he wanted to hear a crazy story. I told him what had happened and how I was so full of awe for God. He took it all in, seeming to not want it to end so I asked if he wanted to come to the Lord. He said yes and we prayed.

When I made it to just outside Bakersfield on the I-5, I checked into a motel for the night. In the middle of the night I sensed the presence of The Holy Spirit like never before. I was being washed in His love. It was so incredible. The room seemed to have an aura. It lasted all night, coming in waves; I was in the presence of God. I was riding a super high when I went for breakfast. I asked the black lady who served me if she was a believer. When she said yes I told her what I had experienced. She laughed as she told me that there was revival going on all over town and that several people were having similar meetings with God. I went to LA and back home on a cloud.

The last truck I bought was the one with the most problems. I was half way between Los Angeles and Sacramento when the head gasket blew out. I had just passed Harris ranch. It was the middle of summer with temps between 115F and 120F. The tow truck hauled me to the Texaco station that was on the Harris Ranch property. It was Friday afternoon. They said they would repair it over the weekend. I checked into a cheap motel across the road where there were a couple of restaurants. I tried to go to the pool, but the water was so hot it made you sick. I spent the whole weekend locked in the air conditioned room. I was in prison. I would go for a meal and then scamper back to the cool room. By Sunday night I hated California, especially this desert.

Monday morning finally arrived, so I checked out and hurried to retrieve my truck. When I got to the station I noticed a yellow ribbon around the gas pumps. I went over to where I could see my truck. The motor was in the cab but in pieces. I was at a loss to understand what was happening. A man in a suit approached me asking if that was my truck. He told me that the station had been seized by the California tax dept. over the weekend. I was screwed. A bigwig from Harris ranch came over and apologized to me. He said they would move the truck to another shop and cover my costs for the delay. I can't remember the next four days as I was stuck in an eight by eight room. The longest four days of my life finally ended when I got on the road at about four pm Thursday. I headed towards Sacramento and cooler weather. I had gone about 200 miles when the transmission dropped out. It really did. It simply stopped, leaving me without any gears. I was in shock. I put my head in my arms and cried out to God.

After I got it together I called on the CB for help. A semi pulls up and I jump into the cab of a possessed man. I have never seen a person so high. His eyes were as big as apples. He talked like a machine gun. This was my first experience with someone high on speed. This guy was so blasted that I was taking my life into my hands by taking a ride with him. He told me there was a truck stop ten miles ahead and so I went there with him. We made it to the truck stop and they called for a tow truck for me.

We towed my truck and trailer to a town about fifty miles north. I found a hotel and crashed. In the morning I found a shop that actually had a used transmission for a 350 Chevy. It only took a few hours to install and I was home two days later.

The truck business ended when a guy from Texas showed up at Frito-Lay and bought all the remaining trucks for cash.

I was at home one evening a few months later when the phone rang around seven pm. It was Dennis Joiner. He was calling from Toronto where they had liquidated a huge warehouse of giftware. It had been a ten million deal and it was almost finished. There was about 1 million in wholesale value left. They had been open to offers from the Toronto dealers, but they didn't show any real interest. The best bid they had been offered was ten cents on the dollar. Dennis said they would back me if I wanted the deal for that price. Patsi was use to me making snap decisions, but when I hung up and told her I was flying to Toronto later that night, it took awhile for her to get her head around it.

I took the red eye and landed in Toronto around eight am. I picked up a rental car and headed north. The deal was about an hour out of town. I went to the warehouse to see just what I was into. It was unbelievable. It looked like I would never be able to get it all to Vancouver because there was so much. Row upon row was filled with stock from the floor to the forty ft. ceiling. There were over 5,000 different items all in quantity, including huge pieces of brass, carved wooden animals, and porcelain dolls. It is hard to imagine what it must have looked like when the Joiners started on it.

It took a week and six semi trailer loads to get the stuff to Langley, where I had rented a warehouse. It had been loaded without any order so when we unloaded it we simply piled the boxes up and up until we had stacks twenty ft. high. We would just get one truck unloaded when the next one would arrive.

I called every guy in the business I knew. I was selling the stuff for half of wholesale to the dealers. Guys were coming back for load after load. We had rented a store in the front of the warehouse where we were retailing at wholesale prices. It turned out to be the best deal I have ever had. I paid off Joiners in a little over a month, with so much product left that I was still selling it years later.

I was working hard running the White Rock store and now we had the second one. We also needed more space so I rented a warehouse to keep the new furniture until it went on the showroom floor. One evening I got a call saying a load of mattresses were going to be delivered in an hour. The warehouse was full. There was no room, so I gave the driver my home address to load up the garage. I went out to the road to guide him in. It was a semi with a forty ft. trailer. He decided that he wanted to back in our 250 ft. driveway. The road out front was a four lane hwy. There was an area in the middle of the road, just in front of our entrance, that was painted yellow and safe to stop in. We are at the top of a hill so I went to the south side to ensure that no one was coming up the hill as the driver started to back into the driveway.

The trailer was white and it was close to dusk. The trailer was about five ft. into the driveway when I heard a squealing of brakes. It was the scariest thing I have ever heard. It lasted for a couple of seconds ending in a huge crash. A car had run under the trailer. I went into shock as I ran around the truck to see a car buried up to the steering wheel. I knew someone had just been killed. I ran into the house to call an ambulance and grab some blankets. As I made the call the ambulance driver answered saying, “It is OK, Ken. We are here already.” They had been parked at the fire hall across the road. It was a volunteer dept. and they were soon all there. The lady driver didn’t see the trailer until it was too late, but had ducked as she hit it. She was not hurt at all. I saw that there was an empty baby seat in the back of the car. PRAISE GOD! THERE WAS NO BABY IN THE CAR WHEN IT HIT! I was held twenty percent responsible for the accident by my insurance company. The other eighty was split between both drivers.

Chapter Ten

Llama Llama Ding Dong – It's A Farming We Will Go

As another year passed, we again had to create farm income. I knew I didn't want to raise cattle again, but we had to generate an income of a minimum of $2500. That spring I saw an ad for a llama auction that was going to be held at Henry Block's farm in Langley. Henry is one of the most successful businessmen in Canada. He and his brother had started and run Block Brothers Realty, with offices all across the country. Henry was very active in the Christian community as a major supporter of Campus Crusade for Christ. I decided to attend the sale, just to see what it was all about.

There were these long necked woolly animals lining up for auction. As each one was sold the prices kept getting higher, $12,000 for one, $15,000 for another. On and on it went. I watched Henry and he was buying like crazy. I trusted him and if he saw this as a good investment, who was I to disagree. As the sale was slowing down I raised my hand to bid. I bid 7,000 then 8,000 then 9,000 and finally paid $10,000 for a female with a guarantee that she would be bred and would deliver a live cria (llama language for a baby).

As soon as I had bought it a guy comes up to me. He was a ring man doing just as I had done in the car auctions. He asked which one I was going to buy next. When I said that I only wanted one he laughed and said that I had to have at least two. They were a herd animal and didn't do well without company.

The one I had bought had to go back to Alberta for breeding. There was another auction in July at Red Deer so I went to Alberta for the auction and I bought a low end male. There were llamas selling for ridiculous prices with most prices in the twenty to thirty thousand dollar range. One male sold for a Canadian record of $78,000. I met this couple from a small town outside of Red Deer who had a llama consigned to the sale. Their llama was one of the nicest looking animals in the sale. It sold for major money. They told me they had one at the farm who was just as nice as the one they had sold and with the same blood lines. They sold "Privity" to us for $17,000. Llamas became a part of our lives for the next twenty years. We sold Privity's cria for $20,000 two years later.

The availability of retail rental space in White Rock was in short supply, which created a demand. We were using 4000 sq. ft. of the space on the corner of the property that the Joiners had bought. Dennis, who had bought Blake's portion of the property, gave me notice of a substantial rent increase. I reduced the size of the store for a few months, but it didn't bring in enough income. I had the temporary store in Langley that was doing well, so we decided to make the move. Goodbye White Rock. Karen tried to keep a store going on her own at the old location but had to fold after a year and came back to work with us.

I found an old car dealership lot in the middle of Langley. It had been empty for a long time so rent was cheap and many days of cleaning and painting made it look good. It also had a central location. It was about twice as big as the old store, which meant I needed more stock. I had been to a closeout/liquidation trade show in Las Vegas a few years earlier. There were companies who bought and sold business closeout inventories from all over the US. When I had been there before there were many booths wanting to sell their samples on display. They would send samples of all the goods they had available to Las Vegas and have their salesmen take orders.

I drove the truck and trailer down without any promise of being successful. You had to arrive the day before the trade show started and walk around to all the booths asking if they wanted to sell their booths. I wasn't big enough to buy quantities of their stock, but the booth samples worked for me. It was great for them because they would rather sell the samples in Las Vegas than have the hassle of packing it all up and paying shipping costs to return them to their home location. We would pay an average of fifty cents on their wholesale dollar. That would mean that after expenses and exchange on the dollar I would land it at the store in Canada for a dollar. Because it was all discounted product, added to the fact that everything was about double the price in Canada I could make a good profit.

The first trip worked out great and we more than doubled our money. There were four shows a year so I would be spending a lot of time in Vegas. There was also a show every six months in Reno. It was a lot closer than Vegas, but there weren't as many booths available. I was better prepared for the second trip with t-shirts silk screened, "CASH 4 BOOTHS 1-888-CASHKEN." and flyers to leave on tables if I was there before they had started to set up.

We became a force in the booth buying business. We had major competitor who had been in the business for a number of years. He was ticked that a young start-up was trying to steal his business.

The business worked in two parts. We would buy the booths the first two days and then wait another five days for the show to end. Then we would pack up the goods on pallets, shrink-wrap and load them onto a truck. I would buy up to twenty booths at a show and so after the first trip I started to order fifty three foot semitrailers to ship my loads.

During the five days I would go all over town, picking up loads of cardboard boxes to use for packing. I needed help loading as we had to clear out the entire inventory in a matter of hours. I got in contact with a Spanish speaking church in town where I found a young leader who took on the challenge of supplying workers for me. It all worked out, but it took a lot of effort.

I was in Las Vegas for about seven or eight days at a time, by myself. God had delivered me from promiscuity but not from slot machines. I would spend hours watching those reels spin. Never for much money, but I was addicted to the noise and anticipation.

I bought booths for about two years, having success, until our dollar sank to about sixty two cents American, which took out any profit.

During my time there I had some real God encounters. I was having breakfast one morning when God said to me to tell the people next to me that their daughter Carol will be all right. It had to be God. Why else would a thought like that come into my head? I slowly walked over to their table and asked, "Do you have a daughter name Carol?" They said, "Yes, why?" I simply told them that I was a Christian and felt led to tell them what I had heard. I left them stunned and I don't know what happened, but I am sure that they called their daughter. I prayed that all was well, but will never know until I get to heaven.

On another occasion, I saw an ad in a newspaper that the gospel group "THE MIGHTY CLOUDS OF JOY" were doing a concert on Saturday night and were going to have a competition at a small theater on the Friday evening to find an opening act. I showed up on the Friday and had one of the best times of my life. The place was full of spirit filled believers, singing along and cheering their favorite group on. We were all in the aisles, dancing as each group tried to win the coveted gig. I was one of only three white people in the building. I met the white couple. The woman was the convention manager at Bally's Hotel. At the end a group was chosen. The Saturday show was a sell out. I will always remember being in the midst of hundreds of sold out Christians, being in touch their God, all at one time, all in one place. It was one of the best times in my life.

On another day, I was waiting outside the Sands convention center for my workers to show up. Inside there was a coatcheck where I could see the guy who ran it looking kind of sad. I watched him for a while and finally went in to ask him what was wrong. He was hesitant to talk but started to tear up as he told me that he and his wife were splitting up. He said he had left that morning and wasn't going back. My people still hadn't shown up, so I just kept listening to him. When he went silent I asked if I could pray with him. We prayed together. He asked for God's help in the situation and I asked for wisdom on how to help them. In the end I asked where his wife was at that moment. He said at home. I simply suggested he call her. He did and as I left I saw him on the payphone, crying his eyes out. He gave me big thumbs up. My people arrived so I had to go to work

I met many people during that two year spell. I shared my faith with a few and prayed with some others. Sin City is home to a lot of believers. I know. I met a lot of them. Dealers, dancers, cocktail servers, and laborers are often believers. You never know who is sitting across from you as you live your life.

Chapter Eleven

Two Plus Two - "We Are Family"

We were totally committed to our church family. It was far more than just going to church on Sunday mornings. Our social life was centered around this group of believers. We had a home group that met in our home on Wed evenings. There were four couples on a regular basis with others coming and going over time. We did life together.

At Christmas time each year we had a huge church party with everyone participating. We had a meal followed by entertainment. Lots of singing, but the best were the comedy routines. Pastor John always did a Mr. Bean routine with my friend Elwyn playing the straight part. It was so much fun as we all laughed our heads off.

At the 1991 party I met someone who would change my life. One of the families who came to our home group regularly had adopted four Haitian children over the previous few years. This couple had raised their biological children, who were all now adults, and we're giving the rest of their life to these orphans. On this evening they brought their newest son, number five, to the party. I fell in love with this little two year old that night, with him spending the evening in my arms. I had so much respect for Sandra and Albert Knopf for their sacrifice. They were both in their fifties and working to support their growing family. At the end of the evening I told Sandra that we would pay for her next trip to Haiti.

We went back to doing life until about six months later when Sandra knocked on the door, informing me that she was off to Haiti in a couple months. She was going with Lyza, our counselor, to help at the orphanage. I wrote the check and wished them well.

They started to meet together to plan and pray for the trip. During one meeting they had a sense that God was saying that Ken and Patsi should adopt. The thought of kids had crossed our minds about a year earlier when we considered helping raise a family of four foster kids. We knew their grandparents. The mother was a single parent with drug addictions. We met with the social worker and she changed our mind. When Sandra and Lyza came to us with this word, both of us said the same thing at the same time. "NO WAY!" We had our problems getting along at times, but we were living a very satisfying life with long holidays whenever we wanted and I loved my life in business. So when the idea of adoption was raised, I said that unless it was God who showed me that He wanted us to adopt, it wasn't going to happen. I needed a way to ask God. I decided to do a fleece (a religious way to test if this is God's will). I told them that if there were two sisters for adoption we would take that as a sign it was from the Lord. To myself I added that girls were to be aged six and three. I made it tough to fill, just to make sure it was Him.

Sandra and Lyza went to Haiti and returned three weeks later. On the following Sunday morning, Lyza spoke about their trip, focusing on a little girl they had met in the hospital. This child was so undernourished she needed to be hand fed. She had a balloon that she asked the nurses to blow up. None did, so the head of the orphanage, Gladys, reached over and caressed the little girls head, took the balloon, and blew it up for her. The child smiled with such a simple joy that Lyza and Sandra both cried. We had all been affected by Sandra and Albert's sharing their lives with their Haitian kids and now, hearing about this little girl, we were all wiping the tears from our eyes.

After the service Lyza came up and told me that she and Sandra wanted to see me. Patsi wasn't well that morning and had stayed home, so I met with them by myself. They told me about the trip and said they may have found the girls I asked for. They reached in an envelope and pulled out two pictures, putting them in front of me. I looked down at these little girls and my heart broke. They said these girls can be your daughters. I cried. The girls were sisters aged three and six.

When I got home I asked Patsi to come into the office where I played a tape of Lyza's message. I then took the pictures out and put them in front of her saying they could be our daughters. We were in this huge home and crying our eyes out. When the emotion died down, reality started to take over. How do we do this? How much would it cost? How would our lives change? Fear took over my thoughts as I found every reason that said that this was impossible.

The girls had been taken to the orphanage because the grandmother, who was raising them for the mother, couldn't provide for them anymore. The pregnant mother had ten children. The father was only home often enough to keep her pregnant.

The girls were only to be in the orphanage temporarily but were soon put up for adoption when the mother realized that she could never raise them. To give the girls a chance for a better life meant being willing to give them up for adoption. Talk about sacrifice. Esther, the three year old, had been put into the nursery while Jonie was in the juvenile section.

A family from Basil, Switzerland had committed to adopt Esther. Jonie was too old to be adopted, as the age limit was five, so she was to be raised in the orphanage until she was old enough to be on her own. While Lyza and Sandra were there, Esther had been brought over to the Juvenile section. As she entered the yard she saw Jonie and ran to her. The girls were hugging and crying with such joy at finding each other.

Isn't it ironic that Lyza and Sandra just happened to be in the yard to witness the reunion? When Gladys told them about the plan for Esther being adopted to Switzerland and the dilemma she now had, my words about two sisters came to their minds. They told Gladys they might have the answer.

We had to make up our minds in three days. It was insane as we vacillated back and forth. Patsi's family thought we were nuts as did some of our friends. Of course anyone from the church encouraged us.

The day before we had to give our answer, I was driving home after work from Langley when I heard THE VOICE say "NO GREATER LOVE HATH A MAN THAN TO LAY DOWN HIS LIFE FOR ANOTHER." (JOHN 15 :13) I always had thought that referred to someone falling on a grenade in a war or somehow losing your life to save others. It came to me that it said giving up your "life", not your death. It meant to live for someone else. I drove the final mile home and told Patsi I was in. We held each other as we called Lyza with the news.

The adoption program was put in process. It included a substantial payment to the orphanage. We got a deal because we took two girls. Some friends have said that it was because I bargained with them as I do in business, but alas no. We were told how much and we paid it.

It took nine months from the day we said ok to when they arrived. We had to fill out 100's of pages of forms for both countries' governments. Everything we did had to be translated into Creole (the Haitian language) before being sent to Haiti. Everything cost more money. We had to be approved by the British Columbia government which entailed attending meetings with a private counselor who had the power to put a stop to everything. We went through hoop after hoop until it came time for them to travel to Canada. Gladys traveled with the girls as she wanted to come to Canada to visit the church's that sponsored her. We just paid the airfares. In the last week there were so many foul ups at their end. It seemed like we would get call after call from the Haitian lawyer saying that we needed to pay this account or this person to get another paper stamped. I am sure we were just being scammed, but there was nothing to do but pay and pray.

Finally they left Haiti on the twenty forth of August 1993. They flew to Montreal where they stayed the night and came to Vancouver the next day. There were a lot of us at the airport when they came down the stairs in the arrival area. They were thin and small, wearing matching red dresses that a lady at the orphanage made for them. Each had a plastic bag with a toothbrush, a change of underwear, and a book titled "How to Speak Creole in no Time". They came into the middle of a group of excited adults not knowing who anyone was. Jonie was kind of aloof for the first few days while Esther was a typical three year old, cuddly kid. Our lives were never to be the same again.

Patsi's mom had one of the bedrooms while the girls shared the other for the first year. Jonie was seven by the time she arrived. We put her in grade one, holding her back a year so she could have a chance to learn the language and adapt to her new life.

Patsi adapted to motherhood incredibly well with only a few small breakdowns. She had lots of help from Sandra, Lyza, and her mother.

Black hair was the one of the biggest problems for her, which she discovered the first night. She bathed the girls that night, removing the little twists that were all over their heads. As she did the hair exploded in front of her into these huge Afros. Patsi was overwhelmed, but the problem was soon solved with multicolored bows and barrettes that the girls loved.

Jonie's class contained thirteen girls and no boys. They all gravitated toward her and she soon came out of her shell. I spoke some French so she and I communicated for the first few months like that. But both girls were so smart that they learned English by Christmas.

As Jonie blossomed in school, Ester bonded with her mother. I was so proud and happy with all the love in our home. Patsi and I seemed to have more patience for each other, but we still had the same problems with my anger and her stuffing her feelings, it was just hidden for awhile.

The first year went by so fast and it came time for Esther to go to school. After the first two or three weeks the teacher came to us saying Esther just wasn't getting it. She was falling behind very quickly. She suggested that we get her eyes checked.

Patsi booked the appointment. I often sat with Esther in my lap, reading to her. She would put her face up close to the book, but I thought that it was normal. The day of the exam came and we found out she was as blind as a bat. She had a strong astigmatism in one eye and poor sight in the other. They told us they could correct it, but she would need real thick glasses for a few years. We ordered the glasses and waited a week for them to arrive.

The four of us went to optometrist's office. They had us all in the room when they put the glasses on Esther. She let out a yell and then said, "JONIE, LOOK AT MY LITTLE FEET!" She had never seen her feet before. It was just like the blind man that Jesus healed. Everything was new to her. Patsi and I along with all the office staff and the doctor were all in tears as we experienced this together. It was one of the greatest moments in my life.

Esther went back to school the next day. Lidia was not only the teacher, but the wife of my friend Ryoichi who was one of our pastors. She took the time to help Esther to catch up. Esther was right on schedule by Christmas.

By then we were very involved in the llama business. Each of the girls had different chores around the barn. Jonie was to feed the llamas oats each day. She had to take a pail of oats into the field and dump it in a few spots to spread it out so they all would get some. On one occasion, she forgot to dump a bit as soon as she got in the field, so the llamas started to follow her, trying to get at the pail she carried. The closer the llamas got the faster she would run away. It was a Catch 22 moment. Jonie was screaming, Patsi was yelling at top of her voice to drop the pail, and I was running to get into the field. She finally let go of the pail and ran to safety. The llamas would not have harmed her. They just wanted the oats. We still laugh about it all these years later.

There were competitions for lamas each year at the Fraser Valley Fair in Abbotsford. We would always do well especially with a male that I had trained to do almost anything. It would walk up and down stairs, under tarps, over creeks. He would back up on command. He was so tame a child could ride him. I would always take first place with him so I let Jonie use him to enter the youth division. She did real well and we have this picture of her with the big ribbon and a smile from ear to ear.

The llama auction in Red Deer was so successful that a guy in BC tried to copy it. He did a sale in 1994. He tried to make it some kind of black tie affair, which offended a lot of the farmers. We were just ordinary people who had some expensive animals. His auction was a minor success and he sold some of the consigned llamas but most remained unsold.

At one of the shows an American breeder told me to sell as soon as I could as the market would fall. The llama market was holding its value because the border was closed to importing any animals from the US. The value in Canada was almost five times that of the states. I didn't believe him and neither did anyone else. We were all blind and wanted to stay that way.

As an auctioneer, I knew I could do a better job than the other guy, so Patsi and I decided to hold a sale ourselves. It was to be in May of 1995. We choose Chilliwack as the site. We rented the hockey arena and started to promote the sale. I attended every event in Alberta and BC. We sent invitations to every llama farmer in Canada. We charged a 500 dollars entry fee and a ten percent commission. We sold advertising in the catalogue, which covered the $5,000 it cost to produce it. It took one year of work but when auction day came, we grossed $350,000. We also sold every llama as it was an unreserved sale.

Our prices were lower than Red Deer and their prices had been lower than the year before, so there was a downward trend happening. Some people refused to believe it, but one farmer was smarter than the rest of us and held a dispersal sale at Henry Block's farm soon after. Those prices were lower still.

I had about forty llamas by then and decided it was time to make a move. We held another sale in 1997 for ourselves with just a few consignors. I did the sale and was determined to not take any animals home. I had a male who had one of the best bloodlines in the country and had produced a young male, which I was going to use as a stud. I decided to put him up first to set the standard for the sale. There was a buyer who had decided to get in the llama business at that time. Bad decision, but he was there to buy and bought the male for $5,000 (it would have sold for $20,000 two years earlier). I sold sixteen of my llamas, all I wanted to sell, to him for $25,000. Only one of the other consignors wanted to sell when they saw the prices.

The llama market fell like a rock after that just like it had with ostriches a few years before. It has never recovered. Some llamas were eventually sold for fifty bucks apiece at the local livestock auction. Over the time I think I broke even on the venture, but I was able to keep the farm status for property tax purposes for over twenty years, saving upwards of 100 thousand dollars.

I had met a man who decorated his 10,000 square foot house in an over the top fashion every Christmas. Ray used many thousands of lights and any new, outdoor decorations, especially if they were animated. One day in early November Ray asked if I would lend him a llama over the holidays. He wanted to make a display of the stable with a baby Jesus and have the llama standing nearby. He lived on a city street and he was going to make the stable in his garage. I lent him the llama and he made headlines in the local paper again that year. Ray wanted to thank me and offered the use of his cottage at Christiania Lake, which was about two hundred miles east of Vancouver. Patsi and the girls were all excited we set out for a long weekend on the lake. After a hot four hour drive we arrived only to find the cottage was not on the lake as we had anticipated but was next to the main highway and in need of much repair. We settled in but I knew I had to find some way to cheer everyone up. I spied a speedboat out back, loaded on a trailer. I called Ray and he said if I could start it I could use it. After an hour of frustration I hooked the dead motor and boat to my car, towing it to the local repair shop. Two hours and $150 dollars later the boat was running. I went home and loaded the family. Patsi couldn't swim so was very apprehensive but went along after we all had life jackets on. I launched it and started out real slow until Patsi was calm. She actually started to enjoy the ride, even as I speeded it up a little. In fifteen minutes or so we were at top speed running straight up the middle of this long glacier lake. We were in wonderful sunshine and surrounded by snow capped mountains. It was paradise. In the distance, off to the right, I could see the sky was a little darker but nothing to worry about. As we neared the far end of the lake I felt a little hesitation in the motor. I tried to ignore it but there was soon another and another. Oh boy this was not going to be easy to tell Patsi but just as I went to tell her, the motor quit. It was dead, real dead, stone cold dead. No spark dead. I was soon to be dead too. In the quiet after the motor quit I heard thunder in the distance. As I looked up, the mountains in east were encompassed by dark clouds and moving directly over the lake. This time I saw the lightning that was soon followed by the crash of thunder. All over the lake boats were heading for the safety of shore leaving one solitary, sixteen foot boat alone in the center of this liquid highway. Patsi started to get very excited, grabbing an oar and waving for help but no one was too come in the center of a lightening show. The rain hit in torrents as if dumped from a bucket. The lightning was heading right for us but no persuasion from me could keep Patsi from waving her paddle. She was yelling "HELP" over and over. I finally had to take the paddle, telling her to sit low as she was going get us fried. The girls were huddled up in the dark, under the deck, and all I could see was the white of their eyes, big as saucers. I had to calm Patsi as she was so angry that no one would rescue us. The storm passed over us leaving us safe and soaked. As Patsi rose to wave her paddle again, I looked up and as the black clouds opened directly above us, a rainbow appeared, brighter than any I ever seen. Each color was crystal clear. God was just telling us it was all in His hands and under control. A boat soon came and towed us back to shore safe and sound.

On the Saturday morning of the first weekend of August in 1995, I had got a call from my brother-in-law in Peterborough, saying that my mother had had a heart attack. My father had had a stroke two years before and lost most of the mobility on his left side. He had always been very demanding of my mother, but it had become insane for her since the stroke. I think she just wore out at the age of sixty nine. She died later that day.

I flew home the same night. My sister Anne had made many of the arrangements for the funeral already. In Ontario, most people choose to have traditional funeral with a viewing followed by an internment. My mother's viewing was from two to four pm and from seven to nine pm. We were in the room with her body when some people came in to express their condolences. There started to be a line that grew and grew until it was outside the building and then going around the block. I was totally blown away as several 100's of people came in and told me how much my mother had meant in their lives. This happened at both viewings.

My mother had been a member of many organizations and had even formed a charity to provide teddy bears that she and others had made, to kids, when a fire had hurt their lives. She seemed to have touched many people. I was not aware of how loved she was. I was stunned as the day wound down at how little I knew of my mother.

I was both proud and sad. Mostly I was sad that I had been robbed of this knowledge until that day and now could never tell her how proud I was of her. She had had a tough life with many painful moments. She had come back to Jesus late in life so I have the assurance that we will spend eternity together. It only seemed just that my aunt, who had been so hurtful to my mom, had to sit there and watch all these people give her such praise.

Our church was at its peak in the late 90's. Patsi had been hired as the church secretary and was one of the worship leaders. Our home was filled the sound of her learning from her favourite gospel singers. She would practice for hours at a time. She was awesome as a soloist and even better as a worship leader. We had around 400 members with the Sunday service filling all the seats and some of the balcony. One member was Elizabeth Price who was the Canadian President of Women's Aglow and had many contacts among the Christian community. She had arranged for Patsi to sing and me to speak at Full Gospel Business Men's Dinners (like the one where I came to Jesus) to share our story.

This organization had been founded in California many years before by Demos Shakarian. He was a simple dairy farmer whose live had been changed when he met Jesus. He started to have small meetings to create a forum for people to share what Jesus had done in each person's life. It grew to become a worldwide fellowship used to lead thousands of people to the Lord. The meetings were often very charismatic, with a move of the Spirit a normal part of every meeting.

I had attended many lunches with the FGBM in Abbotsford and knew what to expect while Patsi had only had one experience. It was when Demos had spoke at a meeting in Langley in the early 1980's. The auditorium was filled with over a thousand people. Demos was a very quiet speaker. He shared his message ending with an alter call, giving an opportunity for people to turn their lives over to Jesus. Hundreds of people went forward to have Demos pray for them. As he stepped down the steps from stage, this simple man was full of the Spirit of God. The people closest to the stairs started to fall over under the power of the Spirit. As he moved through the crowd everyone in his path fell to the ground like a wave. There were hundreds of people laid out on the floor. It was an awesome move of God but the memory of it caused Patsi to be a little apprehensive of our speaking in this setting in case something similar happened to us.

Elizabeth had arranged for our first FGBM meeting to be in Maple Ridge. Patsi would sing a couple of songs and I was to give a message. It went well, ending with an alter call for healing. Elizabeth and her husband Jerry were there. Jerry came forward for prayer. Jerry had been on a missionary trip to the Philippines a few years earlier where he had been in a severe car accident. He had serious head injuries that cause him to be in rehab for a long time. Whenever we pray for people we make sure someone is behind the person to catch them if they fall. I put my hand on Jerry's forehead and he went down like a log. The guy behind him went numb and just let him fall. He forgot to catch Jerry. Jerry hit the floor, banging his head hard. I went into shock as I bent over to see how much harm I had caused. Jerry just lay there, praying and praising God. I left him there as I moved along the line. I went back to Jerry only to see him up and feeling great. I will never know why God allowed that to happen, but I know He had a purpose. Perhaps that was His way to heal him. We went on to share at several meetings and prayed with many people, some falling, some not but never experienced anything like that again.

A couple from the US, who had a ministry for children, spoke one evening at our church. We had brought friends who had a seven year old son.

I found the service one of the most boring I had ever heard. It seemed to go on forever, only ending when the man asked for all the kids to come forward. All the kids rushed to the front where the man started to lay hands on each kid. To my great surprise, kid after kid fell down under the power of God. I was in awe of what was happening when his wife came up to me, telling me that she could see God's hand on me. She called her husband over. When he touched me on the forehead, I hit the ground like a sack of potatoes. I lay there for a minute sensing God's presence. I got up and started to pray for others. As I laid my hand on them they too would hit the deck. Over and over it went on. I started to pray for kids and they went down as well until I prayed for the boy we had brought. He just stood there not moving. I didn't understand it until it came to me that he had never asked Jesus into his heart. I asked if he wanted to and after he had prayed, I touched him and he was down. What an experience.

Patsi had been having some medical problems around this time. She was having severe pain in her back. It turned out to be her gall bladder and needed to have it removed. Operation day came; I took her the hospital and went home to watch over the kids. Lisa went to the hospital soon after the operation bringing a big bunch of flowers. She was shocked by Patsi's appearance; she looked awful. Hair stuck flat to her head, no makeup and a sickly pallor to her face. As soon as Lysa left the hospital she called to say all was well but informed me of how Patsi looked. I loaded the kids and headed for the hospital. We got a gift at the shop and rode the elevator to third floor, swung open the door to the room. I saw her in the first bed on the right, laying on her side and looking terrible. I knew I had to show that all was well so I bent over and kissed her cheek. Just as my lips touched her cheek Jonie called out, "DAD, MOM IS OVER HERE" I just kissed a total stranger who was a very sick lady.

Chapter Twelve

I Need To Get Something Straight - Me

The girls had been in Canada for seven years now and were doing so well. We were a family like all families with growing pains. The girls had assimilated into their new life with little trouble. But I still had to deal with my underlying anger issues. I would blow and Patsi would stuff. Every so often we sought Lyza's help. Together we would work out the issues as they arose. It turned out that we were just putting bandages over the hurts without actual healing them. It would all come out at the turn of the century.

On December 31, 1999, we went to friends with the kids to bring in the New Year and next century. We all had a good time and so it came as a huge surprise that when we got home all hell broke loose. I left my jacket on the back of a chair, setting Patsi off. She told me to hang it up. I said I would in the morning. Somehow that hit her between the eyes like a bullet. She went off like never before, letting all the hurt that she had been stuffing out all at once. She told me she hated me and wanted out of their marriage a.s.a.p. I was stunned, striking out in my own verbiage. It became a war in just a few seconds as we sunk back into the abyss.

There was no solution to our situation and the house was quiet for a number of days. I was in despair when I heard Patsi say she didn't want to continue and "sure didn't want any more counseling."

We finally contacted Lyza to mediate. We met with Lyza three times with little or no progress. Lyza suggested we meet separately for a while with Patsi starting first. They met a few times with Lyza suggesting to Patsi that she just do something nice for me that week. Patsi said she didn't even like me and sure didn't want to do anything nice for me. That evening, as Patsi was doing dishes, she was telling God how angry she was. She kept muttering until God spoke to her. She rarely experienced hearing Him, but knew it was Him when He told her to do something. He said, "I WANT YOU TO WASH KEN'S FEET." She said no way and tried to stuff it. She was so angry that He would tell her to do something like this. She argued with Him for a while before finally giving in. She got out a huge bowl, filled it with warm water, got a towel, and headed for the living room. I was sitting in my chair wasting time, watching TV. I saw her come in with the bowl and panicked. I grabbed the phone. She told me to put it away, turned off the TV, saying that God had told her to do this. She knelt at my feet, taking off my shoes and socks. As she started to wash my feet tears were rolling down both of our faces. We cried and cried as our pride was washed away. We both asked each other for forgiveness. The Holy Spirit ministered to us both, healing the brokenness inside. We learned to love that night. True love came into our lives because Patsi obeyed God. Our lives changed as we started to live for each other.

The next day Lyza called Patsi to ask how things were going. When Patsi told her what she had done there was dead silence for a few seconds. Lyza was in absolute shock as she heard Patsi describe the events of the previous evening. Lyza told Patsi that she had meant was for her to bake me a cake or maybe to make me a special meal. Never in a hundred years would she have predicted that as an outcome. Only God can heal our pain.

Chapter Thirteen

Heart Attack City

On January fifteenth, 2001 Patsi and I were sitting together in the living room watching some TV. The girls were in bed and all was peaceful. In the midst of the quiet I had this thought that I had to call Marlene's mother and apologize for all the pain I had caused their family. Much like Patsi's word to wash my feet, I really wasn't anxious to do it, but I knew it was the Lord so I picked up the phone and made the call. Adele was taken by surprise when she heard my voice after twenty years. She had never spoken an evil word to me through all the turmoil I had caused. She had every right to hate me but that just wasn't her character. I told her how sorry I was and asked her to forgive me. All she could say was how I had been such a big help when Debbie had died and she said she forgave me. After the call I felt a peace in my spirit but didn't understand why I was told to make the call. I was soon to know.

I got up the next day and started my exercise routine. I have always been a little heavy but carry it well and enjoy workouts that include weights and cardio. On this morning Patsi had taken the girls to school and then gone upstairs, in the same building, to the church office where she was the church secretary.

On this day I used the Nordic Ski Machine, one of the more strenuous exercises, for about 40 minutes. I built up the program until I was really sweating and breathing hard. I finally stopped and I sat on the couch for a few minutes to catch my breath before heading for the shower. While under the water I felt a little pain in my chest that slowly got worse. Then my left arm started to ache. I knew what was happening, but I wanted to deny it. I got out and sat down hoping it would end. I finally knew it wouldn't so I headed for the truck to drive to the hospital. As soon as I got in the truck I started to throw up. I went back into the house, dialed 911, and waited. Because the fire hall is just across the road, I was surrounded by paramedics within minutes. When the ambulance arrived I was strapped in a gurney and heading for the hospital. The ambulance attendant called Patsi at work and calmly told her that I was having a little pain and that she should meet us at the hospital. I was rushed into the ER with several attendants shoving needles everywhere, attaching electrodes top and bottom. A doctor came and asked questions as they drew blood. The monitors didn't show any abnormal activity so the panic subsided. We were told we would have to wait until the blood work came back before I could be released.

We waited for about three and a half hours when they burst into my area and started to push my bed towards the elevator. They told me I had had a Myocardial Infarction or a heart attack. We were heading for the Intensive Care unit where I was again surrounded with nurses and doctors. I was given a shot of a clot busting drug, but it didn't work as it is only of value if used in the first three hours.

I stayed in there for almost a week before I was sent to Royal Columbian Hospital in New Westminster for an angiogram. It showed I had four blockages with one being 100%, which caused the MI. My heart was permanently damaged but not too severely. They told me that they would bring me back later for an angioplasty where they would open the blockages and stent the arteries to restore blood flow to the damaged area.

The days can get really long when you are stuck in an Intensive Care Unit. I met lots of people as they came and left, leaving me behind to wait for the stents. One man came who did not have any family visit him. It was so sad to watch him when all these other patients had visitors. I took to spending time with him as he lay in his bed. I was feeling great by then, up and walking all over the place at will. It was two days before I realized he didn't have legs. The bed was empty just below his waist. Patsi had brought me a little TV to avoid the ten dollar a day cost of renting one. I asked Patsi to get me another one and I gave him mine. We got to know each other over the next few days. When I told him my story of how the Lord had brought me from the depths and set me free, he asked if and how he could get free too. Another soul set free. Wow! They are everywhere. Everyone needs to hear the truth and to meet Jesus.

As I waited I remembered how God had me call Marlene's mother the night before the heart attack. I really didn't understand His purpose at the time but after, when I realized how close I came to death, I see how He gave a chance to repent for the harm I had done. The bible talks about not taking communion when you have something against your brother. We are to make it right before we partake of the elements. I can only believe He had a specific purpose for me to make that call. God knows all things. His timing is perfect.

After another seven days I got the news that I was to be transferred to get the angioplasty done. Patsi and I had been told that the stents would restore me to almost perfect health. Any reports we had read all showed a huge success rate so we were looking forward to a new start.

I was given a sedative and taken to the waiting room before being rolled into the OR. My turn came and they transferred me onto the operating table. There were lights everywhere and the monitors were all on. The nurses were talking in the corner until they came and gave me a shot in the crotch so they could run the wires up the artery and into my heart. I would feel a warm sensation each time they would shoot more dye. The doctor was working away as I stared at him. I was a little stoned as I watched the monitor showing my heart beating. As they shot the dye, I could see all the little arteries light up, showing exactly where the wires were. After a few minutes I could sense frustration in his voice. Soon after he said, "DAMN, I HATE IT WHEN THAT HAPPENS." I knew this was not good, but the drugs kept me calm. They withdrew the wires and unhooked the monitors. I was soon on my way to the recovery room.

As the sedative wore off I asked what was going on. They told me that the blockage was too long to open and they had to stop before they tore the wall in the artery. I was stunned. Patsi and I had just known that I was going to be healed. We believed what they said. They said I was going to be as good as new and now I wasn't. I sunk into a deep, deep depression as I lay on the bed.

I was unable to move for four hours, until the hole they made in my crotch made a scab and started to heal. I finally called Patsi who was driving home from work. We both cried as I told her I was in trouble. I was released the next day and went home for the first time in two weeks. I was sad as I started to live again. I didn't have as much energy as before but could walk and work. We started to accept the situation knowing God would see us through. Life would be a little different, but we still had each other and the kids. Our church family was very gracious and caring.

I would go to bed a little earlier than I used to, but I had no trouble sleeping. On the tenth or eleventh night home, I was sound asleep and an electric shock hit my body as if I had been hit by lightening. I was lifted off the bed about four inches. I landed not knowing what had just happened. GOD IS WHAT HAPPENED. I may have an artery that blood could not pass through, but that didn't stop Him. He made or opened a collateral artery to carry the blood past the blockage and into the bottom of my heart to feed it the oxygen it so desperately needed. A small part of my heart had died, but the surrounding area was still alive. It just needed more oxygen. The new artery provided the blood and I was made well in a fraction of a second. My energy level jumped along with my spirit.

I gained all my strength back and was normal for the next five years. In 2006 I was scheduled for open heart surgery as some more blockages appeared. I really didn't want the surgery. The thought of my chest being cracked open and having them handle my heart was not something I wanted to experience, but I was told that it was necessary. We had bought a new lazy boy recliner for me to recoup in. The surgery was scheduled for a Monday morning, but on the Friday we got a call I had been bumped for an emergency case.

That evening we went for dinner with Ryoichi and Lydia. I told him my fear and reservations about open heart surgery. He told me about a member of their church. He too didn't want the surgery. He had done some research and found a new tool being used in Japan that was able to go through difficult blockages via angioplasty. He found out that St. Joseph's Hospital in Bellingham had started using it and he had the procedure done successfully, being released the same day. Open heart surgery requires 6-8 weeks recovery time.

I was so excited that I called the hospital the Monday morning. They told me to come down to see them and to bring the video of my blockage. Patsi and I showed up the next day. We were taken into an office to meet a young doctor. He was very pleasant as he asked for the video. He excused himself and went to view it.

In about ten minutes he returned with a big smile. He told us that it would not be a problem to open up the arteries and stent all the blockages. He said they could do it the next day. I asked what the procedure would cost and was told is was $25,000.00. We thanked him and headed home to make a big decision. We decided that we would borrow the money and do this rather than have the open heart surgery. I went to see my cardiologist to discuss the decision. When I told him the story, he wanted to talk to a colleague. The end result was the colleague was able to do the surgery for me exactly as it would have been done in the states. I had to wait a couple of months, but the cost was - $0 – nothing! Our Provincial Health covered it all.

I have inherited heart disease from both sides of my family. Every five years or so, I will need a stent or at least an angioplasty to keep me at 100%. I got another stent in 2011. I live an active life, far from what we thought was ahead before God opened the collateral artery.

The business moved on over the years with some highs and a few lows. When the dollar lost its value against the US dollar I stopped buying in the states. I was never able to get back up to that level again. We had to move to a new location when they sold the auto dealership location. While in the new location I received a call from Sears Canada offering to sell us all their clothing returns for ten cents on the dollar. I took the deal and Cash-2-U became a clothing liquidation store. We struggled until I started to buy new clothes. They were seconds, overruns and samples from a number of factories and importers in the Vancouver area.

God seemed to always meet our basic needs, but there were times I needed more so I asked Him for it. On one occasion, I needed the sales for the month to be $25,000. As the month progressed I could see that the goal was in sight. By the second to the last day we needed more than I thought possible but then a large sale put it within reach again. When the last day came we still needed around 1000 dollars. The difference started to shrink as the day progressed so that at closing I thought we would be close. I took the money into my office and began to count. The total for the month was $24,987.00. I thanked God for His provision. I then had the audacity to say why He didn't just do it to the exact amount. HE SAID, "WHY DON'T YOU COUNT YOUR CHANGE." There were 26 days that the store was open that month. Some days there would be 30 cents change while on others, it was 70 cents. The average was 50 cents a day. 26 days at 50 cents per equaled $13.00. It added up to exactly $25,000 for the month. With God all things are possible.

On another occasion, I had placed lots of ads for a one-day sale, asking for $5,000 for the day. It seems crazy, but that was exactly the amount of the deposit that night.

On another occasion, I asked for $1,000 for the day. A bill came in during the day that had to be paid on the spot. I changed my request, adding the $160.00 to what I needed. At closing I took the cash into the office. It was 3 minutes to closing and we were $6.00 short. The last lady was at the till and the doors were locked. Her bill was...guess...$6.00... Crazy! I know that's what happened. He is the God of all our needs.

It isn't always money that He provided. During one of my hundreds of garage sale ventures I spotted a complete set of concordances by J. Vernon McGee sitting on a book shelf in a corner of a garage. I had wanted this particular set of fifty books because of the clarity of the teaching in plain English. I asked to buy them at that time but the owner refused. I forgot about them until about three years later. I again was on the Saturday morning hunt and was getting tired around noon. There was one sale on the list that I had missed but decided to forego it. I then had a sense that God was telling me to go there so I turned around and found the home. As I arrived I saw a man attempting to load a large table into the back of his car. I told him I would give him a hand in a minute as soon as I had seen what was for sale. I thought there must be something good as I believed God told me to go there. I was soon disappointed when I saw nothing and turned back to my truck. I grabbed a corner of the table for the guy only to see that it would never fit. He said he lived nearby so I told him that I would put it in the pickup and drop it off for him. Imagine my surprise as he drove to the house with the concordances. As he arrived, the garage door rose and I spied the shelf with the books. I left with them.

Chapter Fourteen

Church Life Becomes Messy

In the summer of 2000 John and Lyza had decided to take a one year sabbatical after having served the church for thirty years. They arranged for a replacement pastor to cover for them. The replacement pastor had served for many years in a number of churches in the Vancouver area as a lead and associate pastor. John was a very charismatic preacher with many spiritual gifts. The church was a strong Christian presence in the community. John's main goal for the church was unity of all denominations.

The new guy was a change for the congregation, visiting them at their homes on a regular basis. Many members appreciated this approach and voiced it to him. He began to think he could do a better job than John and started to lay the foundation for a takeover of the church.

The year passed quickly with the Clarkes returning refreshed and motivated to take the reins. They had lots of renewed passion and wanted to focus on the new ideas they had gleaned over the year. Soon after their return there was an uprising in the church, led by the new guy. He had motivated a few of the leaders to come along side with him with the purpose of ousting John as lead pastor. This action played its way out over the course of the next couple of months, ending with John and the elders giving him his dismissal papers, but not before he had scooped up a few of the members.

With the end of the coup John started to share some of his new plans. During the first daylong leaders meeting, he showed a video featuring the Jabez Prayer by Bruce Wilkerson. I had prayed almost every day since coming to the Lord, but this shone a new light on how to focus my prayer and to line it up with God's purposes for me. It is based on an obscure passage of scripture where Jabez prayed, asking God to bless him. It goes like this

BLESS ME LORD, BLESS ME INDEED
FILL ME WITH YOUR SPIRIT
INCREASE MY TERRITORY
PROTECT ME FROM THE ENEMY
DO NOT LET ME CAUSE HARM

He talked about how God had blessed Jabez because Jabez had asked for blessings and that it is God's joy to bless us. He taught how to personalize the prayer for our own lives. My prayers, until that time, had been scattered and unorganized. I began to follow the lead of Jabez. Not to use it as rote but simply as a guide. I pray for blessings in my family, for friends, my marriage, and any needs that my friends or I might have. I ask for the Holy Spirit to daily fill me more and more with His presence and to guide me in my thoughts and actions. I ask for wisdom, for Him to increase my territory by creating opportunity to be of use to the kingdom, to guide me to people who need to hear of Him. To open the doors that need to be opened and to close doors to places He doesn't want me to go. I pray for His protection as I go about life, to keep me from temptation and that I can take on the full armor of God on a daily basis. That I not cause harm to anyone and, finally, have wisdom, to be wise about what I say and do, so that I know what could harm His kingdom.

I have followed this guideline since that day accompanied by studying MY UTMOST FOR HIS HIGHEST. I can only tell you that this has helped me to keep my spiritual life in line with what I believe God wants for me. I would recommend this for anyone seeking to get closer to God.

Our church made a major change in 2006 when John and Lyza wanted to step down. The elders had hired a young couple as youth pastors a couple of years before so it was their desire for them to take over. The transition was not without difficulties as some members didn't agree with the decision.

In the end their plan went ahead and they were placed in charge with John and Lyza acting in a supporting role. Many changes took place in a hurry. The first was a change of name. White Rock Christian Fellowship became Life Church. A new format in preaching and worship followed. Many more people soon left. Patsi was let go as church secretary as the finances were floundering. It never seemed to "get a grip", sputtering for a couple of years, until a bomb dropped. There was a major sin exposed in the new leadership group. The husband was going to step down as his wife had been involved in the failing. At the last minute he decided to stay as head pastor as a single man. The church was down to around sixty or seventy people on a Sunday morning from the 300 or so when John was leading. We were spending our winters down south by then and avoided much of the turmoil. But upon one of our returns home, we were shocked at the disorganization and felt we had to leave. He stayed on for another couple of years but was facing an impossible task and eventually stepped down. There is a mature couple with pastoral experience now running it and have hopes to be able to return it to its glory days.

2006 was also a tough year in our personal lives as well when Norma, Patsi's mom and best friend, died from cancer. The loss Patsi experienced was so great. They were so close as only a mother/daughter can be. She still morns all these years later. My father passed away later in the same year. I had been back to see him a few months earlier. He and I had never been close, but in the last couple of years he started to attend church services in the rest home. During the last time I saw him we held hands and prayed. I had prayed for him for several years and can only hope he made peace with God before he passed away.

Chapter Fifteen

We Run For The Border

Just before the church imploded a couple of new guys had started attending. They both showed up on big Harleys each Sunday. I would watch them leave with their loud pipes, "playing a song to my spirit". I didn't realize how much I missed the freedom of two wheels. I was able to resist until Fathers Day, 2007. As I sat in my chair waiting for the service to start, the side doors opened and they rode their bikes into the front of the church, parking them by the pulpit. I couldn't handle it anymore. I looked at Patsi and said, "THAT'S ENOUGH. I AM BUYING A BIKE THIS WEEK." I had received an inheritance from my father so I had some cash to buy the bike.

I got to know the guys and they helped me to find a 2001 Harley Electra Glide with 9000 km on it. It was seven years old and like new. It took a couple of harrowing months to get back to my riding level of thirty years before. I joined up with the guys who had formed a church for bikers. We met at our building on Wednesday evenings for a service with a ride after. On the back of our leathers, we had a patch showing a cross made of hardened steel. It showed our faith and that we had an edge. Our goal was to represent Christ in the hardcore biker world. We would attend fundraising rides put on by Hells Angels and other 1% clubs.

It sure was a lot of fun but doomed to failure because we tried to be a church for bikers while dictating who could wear the patch. If you didn't ride a Harley, you could attend the church but not be a part of the inner core, wearing the patch. I left after a couple of years. I had tried to change the opinion of the leaders, but wasn't successful.

When Patsi and I started to go to Phoenix for the winter, we bought a home in a complex with over 2000 units. Among the sixty different clubs is a motorcycle club with old guys like me, riding every kind of tour bike made...Harleys, BMWs, Gold Wings and now trikes. For the first 2 years, I would go on three to five day trips and I would leave Patsi behind because she didn't feel safe on the bike. I would try to arrange for one of our girls or a friend from home to keep her company. Last year one of the guys had bought a brand new Can Am (a new type of three wheel bike with two wheels on the front). He had a stroke after only having it for a short time. He tried every way to sell it and lowered the price to where it made sense for us to buy it. I could sell the Harley for about half and come up with the balance. We did it and now we are riding together.

On our first trip we spent a week with eighteen other couples, riding from Phoenix to Vegas, to Death Valley, to Bakersfield, to the California coast, down to near Los Angeles, on to Palm Springs, and then home. We had a great time together and with the others. We now have something that we can do together in our retirement.

We ride with people from all over the US and Canada, guys from every walk of life. Some are wealthy while others not so much. There are car dealers, doctors, lawyers, salesmen, and now one auctioneer. One of the riders is the pastor from the church in our complex. We now have two lives, with two sets of friends, one in Arizona and one in B.C, one in the winter and the other in the summer. What often happens now is we have summer friends who visit in the winter while several winter friends spend time with us in the summer. As one of my winter friends describes it, "We are doing life together"

Our lives as a family have been totally blessed. As teenagers the girls each had about a year of insanity, but we all survived.

I eventually ended up in an anger management class where I saw where anger could take you. There were about twenty guys who had similar stories, most coming from similar backgrounds as me. Some had let their anger carry them to its end; being charged with assault or spousal abuse and having restraining orders placed against them. Many seemed not to hear what they were saying as they blamed everyone but themselves for their problems. It is a real eye opener to realize we are the source of our own pain. Everyone in the world has problems. My anger issue is still there and can rear its ugly head if I am not careful. Not in a physical way but with the use of my callus tongue. I have come a long way from where I was but I find myself needing to calm down before I respond to a situation. I am not always successful and usually end up having to apologize for my reaction. I ask God each day to make me better and not let me cause harm to His Kingdom. Anger is natural response in each person; it is how we deal with it that emotion that shows our maturity in Christ. Patsi keeps reminding me that He is not finished with me yet. Thank God.

God has blessed me in my life. He kept me alive for all those years before I surrendered my life to Him. Patsi and I just celebrated our thirtieth anniversary with a long holiday together in Hawaii. We have learned to put each other first. My life has been full and I am truly a happy man as I get to enjoy my senior citizen years.

Scott turns forty one this year and is a true free spirit, living life by his own rules. Cindy has, over the years, had her problems with me. She has decided for the third time to not have me in her life. It hurts but I have a peace knowing that God is in charge. I pray for them both every day, claiming them for God's kingdom. I have owned what I did in their lives and have asked them both for their forgiveness for the pain I caused. Many years ago I had a long talk with Marlene. I apologized for all I had done to her and her family. I asked for her forgiveness. We don't see each other very often but when we do it is cordial. Her partner, David, has been with her for many years. They appear to have a happy life.

I turned sixty five on a Thursday, the twenty sixth of January in 2012. We were in Phoenix and Patsi had planned a party for all our friends for that evening.

In Arizona, Thursdays are estates sale days. I always get up bright and early, as my addiction for bargains has not diminished as I grow older. I get the list from the paper, spend a while loading the GPS, and hit the road. I grab a coffee and snack as I start the trek. It takes four or five hours to complete the journey so by one pm or so, I'm hungry. On this day I recalled having seen an ad for a Chinese buffet. It had said, "EAT FREE ON YOUR BIRTHDAY." I called Patsi to see if she wanted to come, but she already had had lunch so I was on my own. I went up to the counter to tell the girl it was my birthday and I was here for the free meal. She looked at me with great pain and said, "Sir you have to have ten people with you." I guess I missed that part in the ad. She looked at me with compassion and said that she would give me ten percent off my meal. I was there and hungry so I quickly said thanks and headed to my table. I feasted by myself for about thirty minutes.

I was about to get up when a girl came around with a special plate of cakes for me. I didn't realize it was a gift for me and I passed on the cakes. I stood up to leave my cash payment when the sound system suddenly started to blast out "HAPPY BIRTHDAY TO YOU!" The doors from the back room swung open with a line of waitresses, following the leader who had a cake with a sparkler blazing on top and heading for my table.

All around the restaurant people are looking over at this poor friendless man who is celebrating his birthday all by himself. This all happened in a matter of seconds. I panicked and headed for the door to escape. I got in my car, thought about what had just happened, and started to laugh. I laughed hard and long. I called Patsi and related the story. She was laughing and crying when she said, "KEN, IT COULD ONLY HAPPEN TO YOU"

THE END

Epilogue

God gave me second chance as a father, as a husband, as a man, and I passed. I have to be aware that I have an anger problem. God has given the ability to control it. He showed me my trigger points and I have to be aware when one is breeched and decide on how I will react. He is not finished with me as I still mess up all too often "For we all fall short of the glory of God". We all are growing towards being who He has called us to be. Our decision to follow Him is the start of a life long journey that continues every day. I became a good father, which is not how I saw myself in all those years before. God has answered another of my prayers as my precious daughters both have wonderful men in their lives. Ester and Taise have a son, Atus while Jonie and Shawn have a daughter, Naima with another baby due soon.

Patsi and I love these two wonderful grandbabies that are such an important part of our lives. I am an even better grandfather than I was a father. As much as I have learned to love over the years, I never really understood unconditional love until these little babies came along. I know how much God loves me because I love these little ones without reservation. I just love them period. Not because they have done something to deserve it but because they are my grandbabies.

That is how God loves us all. We can never earn His love. He just loves us unconditionally, no matter where we are or what we have done. All He wants is for us to surrender our lives to Him, confess that we need Him, and ask Him to forgive our sins. He has given me a full and wonderful life, not because I deserved it, but because He is God.

When you hear His call, STOP whatever you're doing and respond. He loves you just as you are. Come now. He will do the rest. I know that this is true. When you hear "TODAY YOU CHOOSE" I pray you say yes to Him. I did now it is your turn.

If you are ready to make Jesus "Lord of your life" today,

Pray a prayer like this from your heart.

Dear Jesus,

I believe you are God.

I confess that I am a sinner.

I ask you to come into my heart today and make me new.

I believe you died in my place

to pay the price for my sins.

I surrender the rest of my life to you.

In Jesus name I pray.

Amen

If you have just prayed, you are now a part of God's kingdom.

The Holy Spirit has come into your heart and has started a work in you. Your sins have all been forgiven. Thank God for what He has done for you. You should tell someone what you have done and find a church to attend. I can help you do that if you let me know where you live.

If you have prayed this prayer or have any comments or questions, please let me know. I would be very glad to hear from you. May God richly bless you this day. Thank you reading my story. Please pass it on to someone who might relate.

Ken

My email address is todayyouchoose@gmail.com

My Thanks

To my wonderful wife, Patsi; I love you. Look what the Lord has done. We have experienced so many trials and difficulties but our God has brought us thru. I am so glad you have my back. We are going to end the race well and together.

To Jonie and Esther for being such wonderful daughters; I am so very proud of you. You have both chosen your mates well. I am so blessed. Thank you for the wonderful grandbabies, Atyus and Naima. They are the joy of my life.

To Lyza Clarke for walking us thru all the darkness, helping us to see the light, for all the hours of counselling and not giving up on us.

To Pastors John Clarke, Randy Emerson and Ryoichi Takeda for always being there when I was heading off track. I now appreciate your sharing those words of correction, even if I didn't at the time. You are true friends.

To Kathy Silvers, Dwight Tachiyama, Doug Bonsteil and Bob Lee for taking the many hours to edit and correct my story.

To all my friends from White Rock Christian Fellowship, thank you for your love and encouragement over the last thirty five years. The race is getting closer to the end. I would not have made it without you

Finally, a big thank you to all my friends at Happy Trails Resort in Surprise Az, who have encouraged me to write down all the stories shared over the many meals and times together.

To any Church Leaders

If you think your church or group would like to hear our story live, Patsi and I would love to come to visit. We always bring a pure gospel message, filled with hope and some light hearted moments as we laugh at ourselves. We focus on the different areas where God has blessed us. How He called me by name when I was so lost, how He delivered us from ourselves, saving our marriage, giving us two beautiful daughters and made us a family. We want to lift up His name when and wherever we are called. Patsi is a talented contemporary gospel singer with a country bent. You will share in her love of worship as she sings from her heart. Just send an email and I will reply right away. Our home is in the Fraser Valley of British Columbia in the summer and in the Phoenix area in winter. My email address is todayyouchoose@gmail.com